Separate
For a Reason

Re-Examining Separation of Church and State in America

Janet Ruth

Unless otherwise noted, Scriptures are taken from THE HOLY BIBLE, NEW INTERNATIONAL VERSION®, NIV® Copyright © 1973, 1978, 1984, 2011 by Biblica, Inc.® Used by permission. All rights reserved worldwide

ISBN: 978-1-7334184-2-3

CONTENTS

Introduction

The first eight chapters of this book were originally written in 2004. That year, the Supreme Court of the United States made an important decision regarding the Pledge of Allegiance and the First Amendment Establishment Clause. Many people hailed that decision as a victory for Christians and a defeat for liberals who seek to remove God and Christian ideals from American public life. The original title of this book was *One Nation Under God*, and it was written to explain that 2004 legal decision and what it meant for Christians in America.

Since 2004, battles over religious freedoms, public expressions of religious belief, and important moral issues have continued, with some of those fights making their way to the Supreme Court. Several new decisions have been rendered regarding the First Amendment Religion Clauses, not always favoring the same side. With each new decision of the courts, it seems that the nation has become more and more divided.

In response to these developments, I offer this updated version of my book with a new chapter at the end devoted to recent decisions of the courts. I would also like to take this opportunity to further clarify my position.

Most people are familiar with the two sides of the Church/State divide. One side believes religion should play no role in the public life of our nation. The other side believes

Judeo-Christian beliefs and morals have played a vital role in securing the peace and prosperity we enjoy and should continue to define our national character. But these are not the only positions we can take.

Christians who argue that our nation needs a religious foundation for its laws and public policies are usually motivated by one of two things (or possibly both). The first is the belief that God desires this nation to be influenced and guided by Christian principles. The second is the fear that our nation and the blessings we enjoy are at risk if we stray from those principles. For the sincere Christian, both of these are strong motivations. But what if it is not God's desire for us to live in a "Christian nation"? What if the New Testament calls us to a very different kind of life? Should we let fear, tradition, national pride, or anything else keep us from fulfilling our true purpose?

I encourage you to read this book with an open mind and a prayerful heart. You may learn something you didn't know about American history. You will probably gain a better understanding of how court cases are decided in the United States and how the Constitution is interpreted. Most importantly, you will be challenged to consider what your role is as a Christian in this or any other nation.

As Americans, you and I have many rights and liberties, but we need to use them wisely, with as much information and understanding as we can gather, and giving our allegiance to whom it has always belonged—our God.

Chapter 1

"Under God" Under Fire

Every school morning in...public schools, ...teachers, funded with tax dollars, have their students stand up, ...place their hands over their hearts, and affirm that ours is a nation under some particular religious entity.

I am an atheist. I don't believe in God. And every school morning my child is asked to stand up, face that flag, put her hand over her heart, and say that her father is wrong.

~ Michael Newdow, in argument before
the United States Supreme Court, March 24, 2004 ~

It is something we, as Americans, have been doing our whole lives. We did it as children at school, we do it at public assemblies, we do it at government ceremonies. Nearly every child in America, from kindergarten on up, can recite the Pledge of Allegiance. It is associated with patriotic pride, historical significance, and—for many—religious belief. It is a practice and a heritage most of us take for granted. At least we did, until June 26, 2002, when the Ninth Circuit Federal Court of Appeals ruled that the Pledge of Allegiance to the American flag is unconstitutional.

This latest attack on religion in America should not have come as a surprise. Prayers in public schools have already been abolished.[1] A state courthouse has been ordered to remove a monument of the Ten Commandments from public view.[2] Another courthouse was ordered to remove a manger scene significantly displayed at Christmas time.[3] Public debate has flared up with each of these court decisions, and Christians have been asking themselves, What's next? Will our state and federal legislatures be prevented from employing chaplains and opening their sessions with prayer? Will the motto "In God We Trust" be removed from our currency? Will we even be prohibited from singing patriotic songs such as "God Bless America" and "The Battle Hymn of the Republic"?

The outcry against the pledge case was loud, but it was not unanimous. When the Supreme Court agreed to review the decision, twenty-nine *amicus* briefs were filed in support of the government, while twenty-one were filed in support of the respondent, Michael Newdow.[4] When Newdow walked out of the Supreme Court building on March 24, 2004, after oral argument before the Court, he was met by opposing crowds, one group holding signs such as "America—It's not just for fundamentalists anymore" and "One Nation Under the Constitution" and the other group singing "God Bless America." Newdow, who was originally surprised by the attention he received from his complaint, responded, "Anybody in the country can uphold the Constitution. What a system."[5]

> ### *Amicus* What?
>
> *Amicus curiae*: Latin for "friend of the court." A person or group who is not a party to a lawsuit (the person suing or the person being sued) may sometimes file a brief to express their viewpoint on the case. Rule 37 of the Supreme Court states that "an *amicus curiae* brief that brings to the attention of the Court relevant matter not already brought to its attention by the parties" may be filed with permission of the parties or by asking for consent from the Court. Considering that a court's legal decisions apply to all the people within its jurisdiction, this practice allows other people who will be affected by the outcome of a case to have a chance to present their arguments for or against a particular ruling.

It turns out, however, that Newdow was not the right person to "uphold the Constitution" in this case. On June 14, 2004, the United States Supreme Court issued its ruling on the case, overturning the Ninth Circuit's decision. Refusing to rule on the constitutionality of the Pledge, the highest court of the land ordered the case to be dismissed because Newdow did not have legal custody of his daughter and could not bring a suit on her behalf. Nor could he bring the suit on his own behalf as a non-custodial parent.[6]

Newdow's challenge failed, but the question he raised is far from settled. What many people want to know is how this sort of thing even happens. Will Newdow try again? Or will someone else who does have legal custody of a child in school bring a challenge against the Pledge? Can one man force his opinion on the whole country? The answer is no—and yes.

The Battle Begins

Michael Newdow's legal challenge to the Pledge of Allegiance began several years earlier. He filed a lawsuit in the United States District Court for the Eastern District of California on March 8, 2000, asking for a judgment against

1) the United States Congress,
2) the United States of America,
3) the President of the United States,
4) the State of California,
5) Elk Grove Unified School District,
6) the superintendent of Elk Grove Unified School District,
7) Sacramento City Unified Schools, and
8) the superintendent of Sacramento City Unified Schools.

He asked that the school districts be ordered to abolish a policy which requires teachers in the public schools to lead their students in the Pledge of Allegiance. He also asked that

The Reach of the Courts

Federal courts, as well as most state courts, operate on a hierarchal system. It's something like a pyramid, with each court answering to all of the courts above it. Each court, moreover, is made up of many judges. In district courts, single judges hear a case and issue a ruling on it, while in the circuit courts three judges decide a case by majority rule, and in the Supreme Court there are nine judges who must reach a majority decision.

At the circuit court level, the decision of a single, three-judge panel is binding on all the judges of that circuit. In other words, the legal issues which are resolved in one case must be resolved the same way in all future cases heard in that circuit. This is called precedent. The court may not disagree with one of its own prior legal decisions, unless review is granted *en banc*. In that case, a certain number of the active judges of that circuit (eleven, in the case of the Ninth Circuit) may rehear a case already heard by a three-judge panel and issue a different decision.

The decisions of a circuit court are binding not only on the judges of that circuit but also on all of the district court judges in the circuit and all of the state court judges in the circuit regarding matters of federal law or interpretations of the Unites States Constitution. When the United States Supreme Court issues a legal decision, it is binding on all the circuit courts, all the district courts, and all the state courts.

the United States Congress and the President of the United States be forced to change a 1954 law which added the words "under God" to the Pledge, and that the 1954 federal law and a California Education Code's reference to the Pledge be struck down as unconstitutional.

Responding to the complaint, the government asked that the District Court judge considering the case to ignore, for the moment, some of the procedural issues—such as whether Newdow could show actual injuries from the laws he found offensive, or whether the President of the United States has authority to change federal laws—and base its ruling on the main question: Does the Pledge of Allegiance violate the First Amendment to the Constitution? A federal magistrate and a District Court judge both considered the matter and answered the question with a simple no, it does not.

The Bomb is Dropped

Newdow appealed, requesting a three-judge panel of the Ninth Circuit Court of Appeals to review the case. But the wheels of justice do not turn swiftly, and it was not until June of the following year that a decision was reached. Two of the three judges, legally representing the entire Ninth Circuit Court, decided that the federal law which sets out the Pledge of Allegiance was unconstitutional, as were any state laws or policies requiring the Pledge to be recited in public schools. The opinion, once made effective, would apply to all the school districts of all the states within the Ninth Circuit's jurisdiction, including California, Hawaii, Alaska, Washington, Oregon, Montana, Idaho, Arizona, and Nevada.

The government quickly exercised its rights and asked for a second hearing on the case by the same panel or for a rehearing *en banc*. The court denied the motion for rehearing *en banc* and issued a new opinion with a few changes from the first. The conclusion was less broad, but still to the same effect, holding that public school teachers leading their classes in the Pledge of Allegiance is a practice which violates the Establishment Clause of the First Amendment, and is unconstitutional.

The Power of the Courts

The United States Constitution, by its own terms, is the Supreme Law of the land (Article VI, para. 2.). No law may be written by Congress or by any state legislature, and no act may be done by any federal or state agent, that contravenes the provisions of the Constitution and its amendments. All judges, both federal and state, must swear to uphold the Constitution (Article VI, para. 3).

If a court decides that an action has been taken in violation of the Constitution, the court may order the government to pay money damages for any injury the violation caused. In criminal cases, evidence obtained by unconstitutional acts might be suppressed so it cannot be used to convict the accused. If a law is found to be unconstitutional, any government agent who later applies that law would be subject to damages or an injunction. The court may not remove unconstitutional laws from the law books. They may only insist, through the threat of legal consequences, that the law no longer be followed.

A Direct Hit

Before reaching this conclusion, the court did make a few important points. First, anyone who wants to bring a legal challenge in court must show that someone else, including the government, has done them an injury the court can make right. This is called standing. Considering the vast power invested in the courts of this country—the power to order damages (money paid for past injury), injunctive relief (telling a person they must do something or cease doing something or face severe penalties), and declaratory relief (determining the rights of individuals and the legality of laws and actions of the government) —access to the courts is limited to those with real injuries or those with rights and interests actually at stake. The court found that Newdow had "standing as a parent to challenge a practice that interferes with his right to direct the religious education of his daughter."[7]

Second, the court informed Newdow that some of the relief he asked for could not be granted. Newdow wanted both Congress and the President of the United States to be ordered to change the words of the Pledge of Allegiance by deleting the words "under God." Under the United States Constitution, however, Congress is protected from outside interference in all areas which fall within its legislative authority.[8] Simply put, "the

The Power of a President

Forget everything you've heard during election-year speeches. The president does not make the laws. The Constitution gives to Congress the power to make and amend laws. The president, through the vast reaches of the Executive Department, implements and enforces the law. The courts interpret those laws as they are applied in individual circumstances, determining whether a law has been properly applied or is itself in violation of the Constitution.

While the courts must wait for a legal issue to be brought before them, the president is free to consult with Congress about what laws should be passed. This is a power which has grown greatly over the years, as the political clout of the presidents has grown. But no matter how much the president promises, argues, pressures, or pleads, there is no guarantee that he can get a majority of the 100 senators and the 435 representatives in Congress to agree with him.

federal courts lack jurisdiction to issue orders directing Congress to enact or amend legislation."[9] The courts also have limited authority to give orders to the president, and they certainly cannot order him to do something he has no authority to do. The president cannot alter federal statutes or make new ones, as those functions are given by the Constitution to Congress. Newdow's request that the Pledge be changed to remove the words "under God" could not be granted. The court's only authority regarding the act was to declare it constitutional or not.

Finally, the Ninth Circuit Court in its amended opinion—issued eight months after the original—decided not to settle the issue regarding the 1954 federal law at all. What the Court decided was that the policy of Elk Grove Unified School District requiring students to be led in a daily recitation of the Pledge of Allegiance was unconstitutional. Since the teachers of Newdow's daughter would no longer be allowed to recite the Pledge of Allegiance in class, which allegedly damaged Newdow's right to direct the religious education of his daughter, his rights as a parent could be upheld without reaching the issue of whether anyone, anywhere, could recite the Pledge as set forth in the 1954 act.

The Explosion

The outcry was immediate. President George W. Bush called the decision "ridiculous." California's governor, Gray Davis, said he was "extremely disappointed" and called the Pledge "one of our most profound human expressions of American patriotism." Congressional leaders called it sad, absurd, wrong, and just nuts. The same day the original decision was issued, the Senate voted 99-0 to condemn it, and members of the House of Representatives gathered on the front steps of the Capitol to recite the Pledge. The following morning, 80 of the 100 senators were present for the daily prayer and saying of the Pledge which opens the Senate's business each day, a patriotic exercise most are usually happy to neglect.[10]

Back in California, Newdow was the center of a less dignified response. His home answering machine quickly filled with messages of protest and outrage. Some people yelled obscenities. Others threatened Newdow's life. The Sacramento police promised an increased presence in the neighborhood, and Newdow was forced to quickly remove all pictures of his 8-year-old daughter from sight in order to hide her identity.[11]

The nation responded in public displays of support for the Pledge. At one Sacramento school, a sixth-grade graduation turned into a political demonstration as the crowd shouted the words "UNDER GOD" during what had always before been a routine reciting of the Pledge.[12] In a Newsweek poll, 87 percent of those polled supported keeping the words "under God" in the Pledge.[13] A later Associated Press poll showed support for the Pledge from almost nine out of ten Americans, and a Gallup poll the following April showed that 91 percent of the public wanted the Pledge of Allegiance to remain unchanged.[14]

That's a lot of people—but it isn't everyone. Of the 100 plus letters received by Newsweek in response to its cover story on the case, more than half of the writers supported the Ninth Circuit's decision, and not all of them were atheists. Some of the letters were from Christians who believe it is best for all of us to keep the government out of religion. One pastor summed up nicely, "[W]e should not depend on our government to require that God's name be said. Nor can we expect government to require that our children pray. It is up to us in the church to teach our children about God, the Bible, worship and prayer. What we can expect of our government is the freedom to practice our faith."[15]

The Fallout

After the Ninth Circuit's initial ruling against the legality of the Pledge, the mother of Michael Newdow's daughter filed a motion with the court asking for leave to intervene. Sandra Banning, who had never been married to Newdow, stated that she had sole legal custody of her daughter and that she did not agree with the suit which Newdow had brought on her daughter's behalf. The court denied Banning's motion to be involved in the lawsuit but did make it clear that Banning and Newdow's daughter was not a party to the case and that Newdow could not represent her interests. Newdow's only basis for standing was that he was a parent whose right to direct the religious education of his child was being infringed upon by his daughter's school.[16]

It was this specific decision which the United States Supreme Court took issue with. On Flag Day, July 14, 2004, exactly fifty years after Congress added the words "under God" to the Pledge of Allegiance, the Supreme Court overturned the decision which found those words unconstitutional.[17] The Supreme Court did not disagree with what the Ninth Circuit said about the Pledge; it merely reversed the Ninth Circuit's ruling and effectively dismissed the case. Five of the nine Justices on the Court agreed to overturn the decision on the basis of standing alone. The Court found no support for the Ninth Circuit's decision that Newdow, as a non-custodial parent, "has a right to dictate to others what they may and may not say to his child respecting religion."[18] According to the Court, Newdow could not legally represent his daughter's interests before the courts, nor did he have any legal interests of his own to defend.

> This case concerns not merely Newdow's interest in inculcating his child with his views on religion, but also the rights of the child's mother as a parent generally and the [California] Superior Court orders specifically. And most important, it implicates the interests of a young child who finds herself at the center of a highly public debate over her custody, the propriety of a widespread national ritual, and the meaning of our Constitution.[19]

What Next?

The Supreme Court's decision to overturn the Ninth Circuit has done little to resolve the conflict between those who want to keep faith in God as part of our national identity and those who want to expunge any reference to God and faith from our civil life. Both sides rely on our nation's history, the American ideal of liberty, and prior rulings of the

Supreme Court to make their arguments. Both sides claim their view will make America healthier, happier, and more secure for future generations. Neither side can escape the fundamental fact that the issue will have to be decided by the courts based on the wording of the United States Constitution.

Does the Constitution require a strict separation between faith and government, Church and State? What did the framers of the Constitution intend, and how have the courts applied their words over the past two centuries? It is these questions that form the battleground between those for and those against religion in America. It is important, then, to understand this Constitution, which is the source of our rights in America, and to understand the rulings of the Supreme Court which interpret those rights. Eventually, though, it is even more important to look beyond the authority of the courts and the Constitution and to consider what God has to say about being a Christian in America.

Chapter 2

The First Amendment

Congress shall make no law respecting an establishment of religion, or

prohibiting the free exercise thereof; or abridging the freedom of speech,

or of the press; or the right of the people peaceably to assemble,

and to petition the Government for a redress of grievances.

~ United States Constitution, Amendment I ~

The controversy surrounding the rulings of the Supreme Court on matters of religion centers on the meaning of the words contained in the First Amendment. What is a "law respecting an establishment of religion"? Does the amendment forbid the government from having anything to do with religion, or does it simply require the government to be impartial between religions? Does the Supreme Court even have the right to dictate to the states what laws they may pass and what actions they may take in matters of religion, since the First Amendment is directed only at Congress?

The Court's interpretations of the First Amendment, including the decision to apply its terms to the states as well as to the federal government, are the subject of Chapter Three. Underlying those interpretations is the question of what the writers of the amendment intended it to mean. Understanding exactly what our founding fathers thought and felt about religion and religious freedom would take an understanding of the whole history of Western Civilization, since the founders merely built upon the thought and experience of those who came before them. They were influenced by the Age of Enlightenment, the Protestant Reformation, the Magna Charta, the fall of Rome, the writings of Greek philosophers, and the Ten Commandments. For our look at the intent of the First Amendment, however, a very brief review of early American history will have to suffice.

Congress Shall Make No Law

In 1776, when the United States first declared its independence from England, the population of the thirteen American states was predominantly protestant. At least eight of the colonies had official churches which were supported by tax dollars.[1] Many had laws requiring church attendance or limiting public office to men of certain faiths.[2] The fifty-five delegates to the Constitutional Convention in 1787 were probably a fair representation of the people of America at the time, including Anglicans, Congregationalists, Methodists, Lutherans, two Catholics, and at least one Deist.[3] Considering the diversity of religious beliefs in America, the drafters of the Constitution knew it would be impossible to prefer one sect or set of beliefs over another.[4] They made only one reference to religion in the Constitution, stating "no religious Test shall ever be required as a Qualification to any Office or public Trust under the United States."[5] The Constitution, unlike the Declaration of Independence, makes no reference to God.

God in the States

Unlike the federal Constitution, most of the early state constitutions made reference to God or religion, either in gratitude for God's blessing or in recognition of the importance of religious principles to guide the people. This list, derived from the state constitutions made available through *www.findlaw.com*, provides a sampling of the religious convictions of the first states:

Connecticut: *Preamble*: The People of Connecticut acknowledging with gratitude, the good providence of God, in having permitted them to enjoy a free government; do, in order more effectually to define, secure, and perpetuate the liberties, rights and privileges which they have derived from their ancestors; hereby, after a careful consideration and revision, ordain and establish the following constitution and form of civil government.

Delaware: *Article I §1*: Although it is the duty of all men frequently to assemble together for the public worship of Almighty God; and piety and morality, on which the prosperity of communities depends, are hereby promoted; yet no man shall or ought to be compelled to attend any religious worship … against his own free will and consent.…

Maryland: *Declaration of Rights*: We, the People of the State of Maryland, grateful to Almighty God for our civil and religious liberty, and taking into our serious consideration the best means of establishing a good Constitution in this State for the sure foundation and more permanent security thereof, declare [this Constitution].

Massachusetts: *Article II*: It is the right as well as the duty of all men in society, publicly, and at stated seasons to worship the Supreme Being, the great Creator and Preserver of the universe.

New Jersey: We, the people of the State of New Jersey, grateful to Almighty God for the civil and religious liberty which He hath so long permitted us to enjoy, and looking to Him for a blessing upon our endeavors to secure and transmit the same unimpaired to succeeding generations, do ordain and establish this Constitution.

New York: We The People of the State of New York, grateful to Almighty God for our Freedom, in order to secure its blessings, do establish this Constitution.

North Carolina: We, the people of the State of North Carolina, grateful to Almighty God, the Sovereign Ruler of Nations, for the preservation of the American Union and the existence of our civil, political and religious liberties, and acknowledging our dependence upon Him for the continuance of those blessings to us and our posterity, do, for the more certain security thereof and for the better government of this State, ordain and establish this Constitution.

Of the first eleven states to ratify the Constitution, five suggested the addition of specific amendments to guarantee individual liberty.[6] As a member of the House of Representatives, James Madison proposed the following language for a Constitutional amendment:

> The civil rights of none shall be abridged on account of religious belief or worship, nor shall any national religion be established, nor shall the full and equal rights of conscience be in any manner, or on any pretext, infringed.[7]

After being debated and amended in the House and the Senate, the final wording was agreed upon:

> Congress shall make no law respecting an establishment of religion, or prohibiting the free exercise thereof.[8]

The wording made it clear that the restrictions in the amendment applied only to the new federal government and not to the individual states.

During debate in the House, James Madison said he considered "the meaning of the words to be, that Congress should not establish a religion, and enforce the legal observation of it by law, nor compel men to worship God in any manner contrary to their conscience."[9] Some of the states had expressed a concern that Congress might rely on the Necessary and Proper Clause of the Constitution to establish a national religion or infringe on religious freedoms, and "to prevent these effects he [Madison] presumed the amendment was intended, and he thought it as well expressed as the nature of the language would admit."[10]

Famous First Words

The Supreme Court has made much of the words in the First Amendment "respecting an establishment of religion." In the pivotal case of *Everson v. Board of Education*, 330 U.S. 1 (1947), the Court attributed these words to James Madison and relied on Madison's work before the Virginia legislature on religious freedom to interpret his intent in writing the First Amendment. This approach ignores the fact that Madison's own proposal for an amendment on religious liberty said nothing about laws "respecting an establishment of religion." These words were added in the conference to work out the differences between the House and Senate versions of the proposed amendment, and it is unknown who proposed this particular phrase.

The infamous words "separation of church and state" do not appear in the First Amendment or anywhere else in the Constitution. The term is derived from a comment of Thomas Jefferson who once wrote a letter giving his own interpretation of the First Amendment religion clauses. Jefferson wrote: "I contemplate with sovereign reverence that act of the whole American people which declared that their legislature should 'make no law respecting an establishment of religion, or prohibiting the free exercise thereof,' thus building a wall of separation between church and State." *8 Writings of Thomas Jefferson,* 113 (H. Washington ed. 1861) (Jefferson's letter to the Danbury Baptist Association).

Thomas Jefferson was not a member of Congress when the First Amendment was drafted. He was overseas at the time, serving as America's ambassador to France. Although he worked closely with Madison on religious reforms in Virginia, there is no evidence that he had any impact on the final wording of the First Amendment. However, his "wall of separation" has had an immense impact on the Court's interpretation of the Establishment Clause.

Separation of Church and State

The First Amendment at that time applied only to the federal government, but the concept of religious liberty appealed to the young states as well. Even before the writing of the Constitution and the First Amendment, the new state of Virginia had done away with its "establishment." At the beginning of the war, Virginia had suspended its tax support of the Anglican Church (or Church of England), then the only recognized church in the colony, and in 1785 the state legislature voted against an attempt to reinstate the tax, even though it allowed tax payers to designate which church or educational institution would receive the tax assessment.[11] The following year, the "Bill for Establishing Religious Freedom," introduced in 1779 by Thomas Jefferson and strongly supported by James Madison, finally passed. In the words of Madison, "'[T]he duty which we owe to our Creator, and the manner of discharging it, can be directed only by reason and conviction, not by force or violence.' The Religion then of every man must be left to the conviction and conscience of every man; and it is the right of every man to exercise it as these may dictate."[12]

Other states followed the example of Virginia. Within fifty years of the writing of the First Amendment, there were no official state churches anywhere in the United States. A new experiment had begun, hand in hand with the experiment of republican government, to see if the Christian religion could exist without the support of civil government. Again in the words of Madison: "We are teaching the world a great truth,…that Religion flourishes in greater purity without, than with the aid of government."[13]

The magnitude of the American experiment was much greater than most people today realize. Since Emperor Constantine made Christianity the official religion of the Roman Empire, religion and politics had been intricately entwined. The kings and queens of Europe, from the Dark Ages through to the American Revolution, ruled through the idea of divine right; that is, they claimed their right to rule came directly from God. Their laws were God's laws, and the breach of civil law was also a breach of moral law punishable by God and the Church. The early Catholic Church supported this arrangement and made good use of it. The breach of a moral law was also the breach of civil law and punishable by the full might of the state.

The Protestant Reformation questioned not only the authority of the Catholic Church, but also the authority of the civil governments of Europe. The combined might of the government and the Church were brought down against the Protestant "heretics," to save the souls of the dissenters and to reestablish the divine authority of church and king. Nowhere was this seen more dramatically than in the torture and executions of the Spanish Inquisition, but it could be found in nearly every European state. The Catholic daughter of King Henry XVIII earned the nickname "Bloody Mary" for ordering the executions of at least 300 English men and women who refused to accept the Catholic religion, and the Protestant kings and queens who followed her did their share to persecute the Catholics and radical Protestants as well.[14]

> The centuries immediately before and contemporaneous with the colonization of America had been filled with turmoil, civil strife, and persecutions, generated in large part by established sects determined to maintain their absolute political and religious supremacy. With the power of government supporting them, at various times and places, Catholics had persecuted Protestants, Protestants had persecuted Catholics, Protestant sects had persecuted other Protestant sects, Catholics of one shade of belief had persecuted Catholics of another shade of belief, and all of these had from time to time persecuted Jews. In efforts to force loyalty to whatever religious group happened to be on top and in league with the government of a particular time and place, men and women had been fined, cast in jail, cruelly tortured, and killed. Among the offenses for which these punishments had been inflicted were such things as speaking disrespectfully of the views of ministers of government-established churches, nonattendance at those churches, expressions of non-belief in their doctrines, and failure to pay taxes and tithes to support them.[15]

Religion and Government

Madison, like many of his contemporaries, hoped to free the citizens of America from the dictates of government in their religious beliefs and practices. At the same time, he hoped to free the government from the influence of a strong national church such as existed in England and nearly every European country at the time. He believed that only through the separation of Church and State could both be strong. However, separation of Church and State did not mean separation of religion and government. The Virginia Declaration of Rights, quoted in part by Madison in his objections to the church tax, stated more fully:

> Religion, or the duty which we owe to our Creator, and the manner of discharging it, can be directed only by reason and conviction, not by force or violence; and therefore all men are equally entitled to the free exercise of religion, according to the dictates of conscience; ***and thus it is the mutual duty of all to practice Christian forbearance, love, and charity towards each other***.[16] (emphasis added)

Not only the states, but also the federal government continued to reflect the religious beliefs of its citizens even after the ratification of the First Amendment. From its first days and continuing until today, the Congress of the United States has employed chaplains and opened its daily sessions with prayer. The first Congress elected under the new Constitution reenacted the Northwest Ordinance of 1787 which granted federal lands to new territories which could be sold to support schools—both public and private religious schools. The preamble to the Northwest Ordinance, written and approved by the same men who drafted the First Amendment, states: "*Religion*, morality, and knowledge, *being necessary to good government* and the happiness of mankind, schools and the means of education shall forever be encouraged."[17]

It was at the request of the first Congress that President George Washington issued his Thanksgiving Day Proclamation of 1789[18]:

> Whereas it is the duty of all Nations to acknowledge the providence of Almighty God, to obey His will, to be grateful for His benefits, and humbly to implore His protection and favor....

> Now therefore I do recommend and assign Thursday the 26th of November next to be devoted by the people of these States to the service of that great and glorious Being who is the beneficent author of all the good that was, that is, or that will be; that we may then all unite in rendering unto Him our sincere and humble thanks for His kind care and protection of the people of this country previous to their becoming a nation; for the signal and manifold mercies and the favorable interpositions of His providence in the course and conclusion of the late war; for the great degree of tranquility, union, and plenty which we have since enjoyed; for the peaceable and rational manner in which we have been enabled to establish constitutions of government for our safety and happiness, and particularly the national one now lately instituted; for the civil and religious liberty with which we are blessed, and the means we have of acquiring and diffusing useful knowledge; and, in general, for all the great and various favors which He has been pleased to confer upon us.[19]

Washington believed that faith in God was not only good for the country but necessary for its continuance. He expounded on this belief in his famous Farewell Address:

> Of all the dispositions and habits which lead to political prosperity, Religion and morality are indispensable supports…. And let us with caution indulge the supposition, that morality can be maintained without religion. Whatever may be conceded to the influence of refined education on minds of peculiar structure, reason and experience both forbid us to expect that National morality can prevail in exclusion of religious principle.[20]

In 1798, John Adams added his own warning:

> We have no government armed with power of contending with human passions unbridled by morality and religion. Avarice, ambition, revenge, or gallantry, would break the strongest cords of our Constitution as a whale goes through a net. Our Constitution is made only for a moral and religious people. It is wholly inadequate to the government of any other.[21]

Even Thomas Jefferson, who most strongly favored a separation of church and state, admitted that a belief in God was a necessary component of a free nation.

> God who gave us life gave us liberty. And can the liberties of a nation be thought secure when we have removed their only firm basis, a conviction in the minds of the people that these liberties are the gift of God? That they are not violated but with his wrath?[22]

The Paradox

The United States was founded on a principle that there is a God and that God gives rights to men which may not be infringed by the government. "We hold these truths to be self-evident, that all men are created equal, that they are endowed by their Creator with certain unalienable Rights, that among these are Life, Liberty and the pursuit of Happiness."[23] This theory of government is different from that of divine rule, where the king, emperor, or pharaoh represents God on Earth and has full authority over his subjects. It is also different from an agnostic or atheist theory of government where the government answers to no greater authority than the strongest of its members and rules by might rather than right.

Of all the rights supposedly given by God, the right to religious freedom was perhaps the dearest to our first citizens. Many of the early settlers fled from the religious persecutions of Europe, seeking the freedom to belong to a religious affiliation of their own choosing. Religious liberty—the ability to decide for oneself what to believe instead of having religious beliefs imposed and enforced by the government—was a top priority for the founders of our new government. The government they created was based on a belief that all men (and women) are answerable first and foremost to God for their moral choices in life.

But there is a paradox in this theory. The paradox is that our liberty, which is based on faith in God, includes the freedom to ignore God's moral law or even to deny his existence. Madison recognized this in his essay objecting to taxation for the churches: "It is the duty of every man to render to the Creator such homage, and such only, as he believes to be acceptable to him."[24] He further argued: "Whilst we assert for ourselves a freedom to embrace, to profess and to observe the Religion which we believe to be of divine origin, we cannot deny an equal freedom to those whose minds have not yet yielded to the evidence which has convinced us."[25] Not even the Christian ideals so important to the maintenance of the government could be imposed by that government, for "Who does not see that the same authority which can establish Christianity, in exclusion of all other Religions, may establish with the same ease any particular sect of Christians, in exclusion of all other Sects?"[26]

This, unfortunately, leads to an even greater paradox; that is, that the founders built their theory of a republic upon a belief in God while intentionally refusing to define any particular belief about God to be correct. Citizens of the United States were encouraged to live by religious principles, but they were left free to identify and interpret those principles as suited their own conscience. They could choose between the strict moral code of the Puritans, the more permissive attitude of the Anglicans, or even the theories of the Deists who sought to understand God through reason and nature and denied the divinity of Jesus and the authority of the Bible. The writers of the Constitution sought to create "a more perfect Union," but on matters of religion the very liberty they fought for demanded that they be allowed to differ.

Chapter 3

The Supreme Court

Our Constitution is in actual operation; everything appears to promise
that it will last; but in this world nothing is certain but death and taxes.
- Benjamin Franklin, 1789 [1] -

It should come as no surprise that the paradox created by the founding fathers should result in some tension and disagreement for those who have, for the last two centuries, attempted to abide by the Constitution the founders created. At first glance, one might see a great disparity between the rulings of the Supreme Court in matters of religious liberty and the actions of state and federal leaders. The legislatures pass laws promoting religion in the public arena, and the president calls us to observe days of national prayer and thanksgiving. The courts, on the other hand, seem to many people to stand out as liberal activists intent on the destruction of all things religious. What may not be obvious is that the Supreme Court itself is often split among those who favor strict separation of church and state and those who favor accommodation and even support of the Christian faith.

Who is right? It is difficult to say, since the founding fathers themselves could not agree on what degree of religious accommodation was appropriate. Then, as now, there were those who wished to see the government offer no assistance or favor to religious institutions or beliefs and those who thought only a strong reliance on God and religious principles could protect and preserve the nation. In its many decisions interpreting and applying the religion clauses of the First Amendment, the Supreme Court has moved back and forth between these two extremes. The Justices of the Court are agreed that the Establishment Clause and the Free Exercise Clause have the common purpose of securing religious liberty. But, as the Court has noted, "it is far easier to agree on the purpose that underlies the First Amendment's [religion] clauses than to obtain agreement on the standards that should govern their application."[2]

The Fourteenth Amendment

For the first half-century of its existence, the Supreme Court had little call to consider the meaning of the First Amendment's religion clauses. Such issues as public health and morals, education, and most areas of civil and criminal law were still firmly in the hands of the states. But in 1861, the face of America changed. Seven southern states started their own revolution and declared their independence from the states in the north. The United States of America were united no longer. After a bloody and destructive war, the South surrendered four years later. The overriding issue of the war had been slavery. The underlying question was *who decides*? Were the states free to make their own legal decisions, even in the case of such a deep moral question? Or was it up to the federal government to make binding decisions in areas affecting our national character and identity?

The 13th Amendment to the Constitution was proposed and ratified before the end of 1865 to abolish slavery and involuntary servitude. The 14th Amendment was proposed the following year. Ratification of the amendment was even made a condition of restoring representatives from the southern states to their places in Congress. The amendment made all persons born in any state a citizen of that state and of the United States and forbade any state to abridge (lessen or do away with) the "privileges or immunities" of any citizen or to "deprive any person of life, liberty, or property, without due process of law."[3]

The obvious intent of the 14th Amendment was to provide to former slaves the same freedoms everyone else enjoyed. The amendment gave Congress the "power to enforce, by appropriate legislation, the provisions of this article," and gave the federal courts the power to oversee state actions which had previously been subject only to state court review.[4] As the final authority on interpreting the words of the federal Constitution and its amendments, the Supreme Court was given broad power to define the privileges and immunities of all American citizens, as well as our rights to life, liberty, and property—including religious liberties.

The First Amendment and the States

The Bill of Rights of the United States Constitution contains specific limits against the power of the federal government to intrude on the rights of individuals. In determining which of the rights is also protected by the Fourteenth Amendment against intrusion by the states, the Supreme Court has considered which rights are "fundamental" and "necessary to the concept of ordered liberty." Not all of the guarantees in the Bill of Rights have been applied to the states through the Fourteenth Amendment, and some of the guarantees, like the Establishment Clause, were applied grouped with other rights and without individual consideration.

In his dissent in *Elk Grove Unified School District v. Newdow*, Justice Thomas expressed his belief that the Establishment Clause should never have been included in the guarantees "incorporated" into the Fourteenth Amendment. He reasons that the Establishment Clause was not a guarantee of personal liberty like the Free Exercise Clause, but rather a limit on the federal government to intrude on the right of the states to establish and support religions. Should a majority of the Court ever accept this argument, all of the Establishment Clause cases previously decided by the Court would apply only to actions of the federal government and no longer to the states. Such a result, however, is unlikely.

The Free Exercise Clause

It seems the full scope of the 14th Amendment was not immediately apparent to the Court, or to the litigants who might apply to the Court to resolve their legal issues. It was not until 1925 that the Court addressed the issue directly, deciding that some parts of the First Amendment—freedom of speech and of the press—are among the fundamental personal rights and liberties protected by the due process clause of the 14th Amendment from infringement by the states.[5] Fifteen years later, in *Cantwell v. State of Connecticut*, the Court relied on this decision to place all of the rights guaranteed by the First Amendment under the protection of the 14th, including the religion clauses.[6] The Court's decision in *Cantwell* was significant for another reason as well, in that it reveals, early on, the disparity in the Court's treatment of First Amendment religion clause cases.

In *Cantwell*, the Court overturned the conviction of a Jehovah's Witness for failing to obtain a permit to solicit funds for religious tracts. Although the law of the state required that any person soliciting door-to-door obtain and pay for a permit, the Court decided the law should not apply to a person whose door-to-door soliciting was an expression of his or her religious belief.[7] Quite some time earlier, however, in *Reynolds v. United States*, the Court held that a member of the Mormon Church in the Territory of Utah could stand convicted of polygamy even though such a practice was required by his religious beliefs.[8]

In *Cantwell*, the Court observed:

> The constitutional inhibition of legislation on the subject of religion has a double aspect. On the one hand, it forestalls compulsion by law of the acceptance of any creed or the practice of any form of worship. Freedom of conscience and freedom to adhere to such religious organization or form of worship as the individual may choose cannot be restricted by law. On the other hand it safeguards the free exercise of the chosen form of religion. Thus the Amendment embraces two concepts—freedom to believe and freedom to act.[9]

In *Reynolds*, on the other hand, the Court found:

> Laws are made for the government of actions, and while they cannot interfere with mere religious belief and opinions, they may with practices.[10]

The Court relied in *Reynolds* on the history of the drafting of the First Amendment and the interpretation given to that amendment by Thomas Jefferson:

> I contemplate with sovereign reverence that act of the whole American people which declared that their legislature should "make no law respecting an establishment of religion or prohibiting the free exercise thereof," thus building a wall of separation between church and State. Adhering to this expression of the supreme will of the nation in behalf of the rights of conscience, I shall see with sincere satisfaction the progress of those sentiments which tend to restore man to all his natural rights, ***convinced he has no natural right in opposition to his social duties***.[11] (Emphasis added.)

The Court concluded:

> Coming as this does from an acknowledged leader of the advocates of the measure, it may be accepted almost as an authoritative declaration of the scope and effect of the amendment thus secured. Congress was deprived of all legislative power over mere opinion, but was left free to reach actions which were in violation of social duties or subversive of good order.[12]

For some time the Court wavered between the extremes of *Cantwell* and *Reynolds*, sometimes finding social duty more important than religious freedom[13] and sometimes providing exceptions from the law for those with religious scruples.[14] Finally, in 1990, in *Employment Division v. Smith*, the Court returned to the ideals of *Reynolds* and Thomas Jefferson, declaring that—as a general rule—no person may be excused from obeying a law "that is neutral and of general applicability" even if the law infringes on the person's free exercise of his or her religious beliefs.[15] While the "freedom to believe" has been deemed by the Court to be absolute, the "freedom to act" on one's beliefs is not.

Congress and the Court

Three years after the Court's decision in *Employment Division v. Smith*, Congress attempted to soften the effects of the ruling by passing the Religious Freedom Restoration Act of 1993. Under this act neither the federal nor state governments could apply any law against a person to prevent them from the free exercise of their religious beliefs unless the government could show the law was narrowly tailored and supported a compelling governmental interest. As far as it applied to the states, however, the Supreme Court found this to be an impermissible restraint by Congress against the states. See *City of Boerne v. Flores*, 521 U.S. 507 (1997).

The Establishment Clause

While the Court considered the limits of governmental regulation of religious practices, it was also required to determine the scope of permissible government aid to religious institutions. In 1947, the Court took its first look at the requirements of the Establishment Clause as applied to the states through the 14th Amendment. In *Everson v. Board of Education of Ewing Township*, the Court was asked to decide whether a public school district could reimburse parents for money spent on bus transportation to take their children to private religious schools.[16] After considering the history of the First Amendment, a majority of the Court held that the reimbursements did not offend the Establishment Clause.

> That Amendment requires the state to be neutral in its relations with groups of religious believers and non-believers; it does not require the state to be their adversary. State power is no more to be used so as to handicap religions, than it is to favor them.[17]

In reaching this decision, the Court made a broad statement about the Establishment Clause which continues to influence the interpretation of the clause today:

Neither a state nor the Federal Government can…pass laws which aid one religion, aid all religions, or prefer one religion over another…. In the words of Jefferson, the clause against establishment of religion by law was intended to erect "a wall of separation between Church and State."[18]

"A wall of separation" became the litmus test for future Establishment Clause cases. Although four Justices dissented from the opinion in Everson, it was not because they felt the majority went too far, but because they thought it had not gone far enough in erecting this wall. The question became what public aid could be given to religious organizations—schools, in particular—for legitimate, nonreligious purposes, and what aid was forbidden aid in support of religious exercises. Thirty-eight years later, Justice Rehnquist examined the confusing results of attempting to define this "wall": "Our recent opinions, many of them hopelessly divided pluralities, have with embarrassing candor conceded that the 'wall of separation' is merely a 'blurred, indistinct, and variable barrier,' which 'is not wholly accurate' and can only be 'dimly perceived.'"[19] It seems that the "wall of separation" had done little more than separate the Justices who had the responsibility of interpreting it.

A Blurred and Variable Barrier

"For example, a State may lend to parochial school children geography textbooks that contain maps of the United States, but the State may not lend maps of the United States for use in geography class. A State may lend textbooks on American colonial history, but it may not lend a film on George Washington, or a film projector to show it in history class. A State may lend classroom workbooks, but may not lend workbooks in which the parochial school children write, thus rendering them nonreusable. A State may pay for bus transportation to religious schools but may not pay for bus transportation from the parochial school to the public zoo or natural history museum for a field trip. A State may pay for diagnostic services conducted in the parochial school but therapeutic services must be given in a different building; speech and hearing 'services' conducted by the State inside the sectarian school are forbidden, but the State may conduct speech and hearing diagnostic testing inside the sectarian school. Exceptional parochial school students may receive counseling, but it must take place outside of the parochial school, such as in a trailer parked down the street. A State may give cash to a parochial school to pay for the administration of state-written tests and state-ordered reporting services, but it may not provide funds for teacher-prepared tests on secular subjects. Religious instruction may not be given in public school, but the public school may release students during the day for religion classes elsewhere, and may enforce attendance at those classes with its truancy laws."

Justice William Rehnquist in *Wallace v. Jaffree*, 472 U.S. 38, 110-111 (1985) (internal citations omitted).

Endorsement and Accommodation

Outside the area of aid to parochial schools, the Court has spoken with a little more clarity. A general rule may be stated that government actions directly endorsing religious beliefs are unconstitutional while government actions accommodating the beliefs of private citizens do not offend the First Amendment. One year after *Everson*, the Court considered a case in which a public school provided time in its regular school day for religious classes, taught by outside religious instructors, to take place on campus for those students who wished to attend. Because the classes took place on school campus and were difficult to distinguish from any other publicly funded classes, the Court found this practice unconstitutional.[20] Four years later, however, the Court upheld a program where students were excused from their public school to attend religious classes off-campus, even though attendance at the religious classes was considered attendance at school for administrative purposes.[21]

In this latter case, the Court noted:

> We are a religious people whose institutions presuppose a Supreme Being. We guarantee the freedom to worship as one chooses. We make room for as wide a variety of beliefs and creeds as the spiritual needs of man deem necessary. We sponsor an attitude on the part of government that shows no partiality to any one group and that lets each flourish according to the zeal of its adherents and the appeal of its dogma…. To hold [otherwise] would be to find in the Constitution a requirement that the government show a callous indifference to religious groups. That would be preferring those who believe in no religion over those who do believe.[22]

The Court would later decide a series of public school cases, finding that the government's actions in each case endorsed a Christian belief. In 1962, in *Engel v. Vitale*, the Supreme Court struck down the practice of New York public school teachers leading students in a daily recitation of the following prayer: "Almighty God, we acknowledge our dependence upon Thee, and we beg Thy blessing upon us, our parents, our teachers, and our country."[23] The following year, the Court would strike down a state law requiring daily reading of the Bible and the recitation of the Lord's Prayer.[24] In the 1980s it would find impermissible a law requiring that the Ten Commandments be posted on classroom walls[25] and another law calling for a one minute period of silence in public schools "for meditation or prayer," finding that the law was motivated by the desire to return prayer to schools.[26] And as recently as 1992, the Court found unconstitutional a school-sponsored prayer at a high-school graduation, concluding that the Establishment Clause "guarantees that government may not coerce anyone to support or participate in religion or its exercise."[27]

Requiring prayers and Bible reading in public schools is an unconstitutional endorsement of religion, but granting access to public schools for private groups is permissible accommodation. High school students must be permitted to use school grounds for religious clubs if the school grants access to other extracurricular student groups.[28] The same holds true for college students.[29] And public schools of any level may not deny access to religious groups such as churches if access is available to other groups.[30] The Court has also been more tolerant of religious displays on public property if the display is made by private groups instead of governmental agencies,[31] or if the display accommodates more than one religious message (such as placing a menorah and Christmas tree together in a public square)[32] or has a commercial rather than a religious purpose (such as placing a nativity scene beside a Santa Clause house in a shopping district).[33]

Perhaps the most surprising Establishment Clause case was not one in which the Court struck down a governmental practice endorsing religious beliefs, but one in which the Court upheld a governmental practice which was clearly religious. In *Marsh v. Chambers*, the Supreme Court ruled that the Nebraska legislature had not offended the First Amendment by hiring Christian chaplains or having those chaplains open their daily legislative sessions with prayer.[34] As the Court stated:

> The opening of sessions of legislative and other deliberative public bodies with prayer is deeply embedded in the history and tradition of this country. From colonial times through the founding of the Republic and ever since, the practice of legislative prayer has coexisted with the principles of disestablishment and religious freedom. In the very courtrooms in which the United States District Judge and later three Circuit Judges heard and decided this case, the proceedings opened with an announcement that concluded, "God save the United States and this Honorable Court." The same invocation occurs at all sessions of this Court.[35]

Comparing *Marsh* to the school prayer cases can only leave one with a sense of wonder at the inconsistencies of the Court's reasoning, as it is clear that the practice of legislative prayer could not pass the tests the Court has long used in Establishment Clause cases.[36] It might even be said the Supreme Court has created a paradox of its own: The government is not permitted to endorse religious beliefs except, apparently, when it feels it ought to.

Official Prayer

The inconsistency between the legislative prayer case and the school prayer cases has not been lost on members of the Supreme Court. Some have tried to explain away the discrepancy by claiming that adults who are subjected to the prayers in the legislature are not susceptible to "religious indoctrination" or "peer pressure," as a child might be expected to be. See *Marsh v. Chambers*, 463 U.S. 783, 792 (1983). But as then Chief Justice Burger quipped two years later, others may believe that "the historic practice of the Congress and this Court is justified because members of the Judiciary and Congress are more in need of Divine guidance than schoolchildren." *Wallace v. Jaffree*, 472 U.S. 38, 84-85 (1985).

It is important to note, though, the Court has not banned all prayer from schools. Students and teachers alike may exercise their First Amendment right to exercise their faith through prayer on school grounds and during school hours. They simply can't do it as a school exercise.

The Debate Goes On

Accommodation—yes. Endorsement—except in the case of state and federal legislatures and courts—no. Such has been the holding of the Supreme Court's Establishment Clause cases for more than fifty years. But a minority of the Court has never been satisfied with this rule. Ever since the earliest public school case, dissenting voices on the Court have argued the Establishment Clause forbids only the actual creation of a national religion and not mere endorsement of religious beliefs or practices. They claim the government may not force any person to pray to God or belong to any religious body, but it may participate in religious exercises and encourage Christian faith. The first school prayer case reflects this argument and the historical evidence supporting both sides.

In his dissent in *Engel*, Justice Stewart chided the majority of the Court for forgetting our nation's strong religious heritage and lists the actions of Congress and the presidents and even the Supreme Court in acknowledging and thanking God for his blessings:

> I do not believe that this Court, or the Congress, or the President has by the actions and practices I have mentioned established an "official religion" in violation of the Constitution. And I do not believe the State of New York has done so in this case. What each has done has been to recognize and to follow the deeply entrenched and highly cherished spiritual traditions of our Nation—traditions which come down to us from those who almost two hundred years ago avowed their "firm Reliance on the Protection of divine Providence" when they proclaimed the freedom and independence of this brave new world.[37]

Justice Stewart's position was fully supported by the opinion of Justice Joseph Story, who served on the Supreme Court from 1822 to 1845:

> The real object of the [First] Amendment was not to countenance, much less to advance, Mahometanism, or Judaism, or infidelity, by prostrating Christianity; but to exclude all rivalry among Christian sects, and to prevent any national ecclesiastical establishment which should give to a hierarchy the exclusive patronage of the national government. It thus cut off the means of religious persecution (the vice and pest of former ages), and of the subversion of the rights of conscience in matters of religion, which had been trampled upon almost from the days of the Apostles to the present age....[38]

The majority in *Engel*, however, doubted that merely excluding rivalry among Christian sects would be sufficient to "cut off the means of religious persecution." In a lengthy review of the history of persecutions which caused many to flee Europe for the hope of religious freedom in this land, the Court stated:

These people knew, some of them from bitter personal experience, that one of the greatest dangers to the freedom of the individual to worship in his own way lay in the Government's placing its official stamp of approval upon one particular kind of prayer or one particular form of religious services. They knew the anguish, hardship and bitter strife that could come when zealous religious groups struggled with one another to obtain the Government's stamp of approval from each King, Queen, or Protector that came to temporary power…. The First Amendment was added to the Constitution to stand as a guarantee that neither the power nor the prestige of the Federal Government would be used to control, support or influence the kinds of prayer the American people can say—that the people's religions must not be subjected to the pressures of government for change each time a new political administration is elected to office. Under that Amendment's prohibition against governmental establishment of religion, as reinforced by the provisions of the 14th Amendment, government in this country, be it state or federal, is without power to prescribe by law any particular form of prayer which is to be used as an official prayer in carrying on any program of governmentally sponsored religious activity.[39]

The positions set out in Engel of both the majority and the minority so clearly reflect the ongoing argument about the reach of the First Amendment's Establishment Clause, that the decision is excerpted in Appendix C.

Chapter 4
The Pledge of Allegiance

I pledge allegiance to the flag of the United States of America,
and to the Republic for which it stands, one nation, under God,
indivisible, with liberty and justice for all.
~ The Pledge of Allegiance ~

Is the Pledge of Allegiance a prayer? Is saying it in a classroom a religious activity endorsed by the government? When we say the pledge, are we making a promise of loyalty to God or only to our country? Do you even have to believe in God to say the Pledge of Allegiance?

Our government says the pledge is not a prayer. According to the government's petition to the Supreme Court asking it to overturn the Ninth Circuit's decision and reaffirm the Pledge of Allegiance, "recitation of the Pledge is a patriotic act—not a religious act…. The phrase [under God] does not compel anyone to believe in the existence of God or recognize religion in general. Instead, it merely reflects the role of religion in the history of the United States."[1] According to an *amicus* brief filed by the attorney generals of all fifty states, the pledge "furthers the high and nonreligious purpose of nurturing active citizens who grasp the virtues of patriotic life and appreciate our nation's distinctive heritage…."[2] Surely no one can seriously believe something as simple as these thirty-one words could lead to the kind of religious persecutions which motivated the writing of the First Amendment religion clauses. Such a thing couldn't happen in this country. Not in this century.

No? How about the last century? How about during the lifetime of some of the people reading this book? The case of *Elk Grove Unified School District v. Newdow* was not the first case about the Pledge of Allegiance to reach the Supreme Court of the United States. Nor was Michael Newdow the first person to be offended by the words of the pledge on the grounds of religious liberty.

A Tale of Two Cases

Sometime in the mid-1930s two children were expelled from a public school in Minersville, Pennsylvania, because they refused to salute the American flag. The salute, accompanied by the recitation of the Pledge of Allegiance, was part of a daily exercise required by the board of education for all public school students and teachers. Because the students were expelled from school, their parents were required to place them in private schools for which they had to pay. The parents sued the school district, claiming that their children were opposed to saluting the flag and making a pledge to it on religious grounds. The case was eventually heard by the United States Supreme Court in 1940 in *Minersville School District v. Gobitis*.[3] The Court, reluctant to interfere with the authority of a local school board, found that the requirement to salute the flag and say the pledge was not an unconstitutional infringement on the students' rights to worship God in their own way. The flag salute requirement was found to be a proper exercise of governmental authority meant for the "promotion of national cohesion" which is the "basis for national security."[4]

The ultimate foundation of a free society is the binding tie of cohesive sentiment. Such a sentiment is fostered by all those agencies of the mind and spirit which may serve to gather up the traditions of a people, transmit them from generation to generation, and thereby create that continuity of a treasured common life which constitutes a civilization.[5]

It was only two children expelled from a small school district in Pennsylvania. Hardly the kind of oppressive persecution the First Amendment was designed to prevent. The nation was still recovering from a costly World War and a devastating national depression. Requiring a few kids to salute the flag was surely no more an imposition on religious freedom than forbidding Mormon men from practicing polygamy or refusing to excuse conscientious objectors from military training, as the Court had previously done.[6] Surely, our public schools should have the right—even the duty—to instill in our children a little bit of patriotism and national pride.

Two years after the Court's decision in *Gobitis*, the West Virginia State Board of Education adopted a resolution ordering that a salute to the American flag become "a regular part of the program of activities in the public schools," and that all teachers and pupils "shall be required to participate in the salute honoring the Nation represented by the Flag."[7] During the salute, the teachers and children were required to recite the Pledge of Allegiance, which at that time did not contain the words "under God." Failure to perform the salute or the Pledge was considered to be "insubordination." The penalty for this insubordination was being expelled from school. Students could not be readmitted to any school until they agreed to comply with the resolution. While expelled, the child was considered "unlawfully absent" and could be prosecuted as a juvenile delinquent. His parents or guardians were also subject to prosecution and if convicted were subject to a fine not exceeding $50 and a jail term not exceeding thirty days.

Certain students were expelled from school and their parents were prosecuted. The students were then threatened that they would be placed by the state in "reformatories maintained for criminally inclined juveniles."[8] All because they refused to raise their hand in a salute to the American flag and pledge their allegiance to "one nation, indivisible, with liberty and justice for all."

Why did they refuse? The Supreme Court had already ruled that public school children could be required to salute the flag and recite the Pledge of Allegiance. But still these children, all Jehovah's Witnesses, refused to comply with the school's command. Why? According to the Court:

> Their religious beliefs include a literal version of Exodus, Chapter 20, verses 4 and 5, which says: "Thou shalt not make unto thee any graven image, or any likeness of anything that is in heaven above, or that is in the earth beneath, or that is in the water under the earth; thou shalt not bow down thyself to them nor serve them." They consider that the flag is an "image" within this command. For this reason they refuse to salute it.[9]

Students were expelled from school and threatened with incarceration as "juvenile delinquents," and parents were criminally prosecuted for teaching their children not to bow down before anything but God. Even if you don't agree with their interpretation of the Second Commandment, you have to admit they were being persecuted by a government of the United States, during the twentieth century, for their religious beliefs. They were not being prosecuted for actions that were, in the earlier words of the Court, "in violation of social duties or subversive of good order."[10] Nor did they claim any right or freedom which would "bring them into collision with rights asserted by any other individual."[11] They simply refused to do an act which to them symbolized subordinating their allegiance to God to their allegiance to their nation.

This time the Court found in favor of the children. In *West Virginia State Board of Education v. Barnette*, the Court overruled its own three-year old decision in *Minersville v. Gobitis*. The Court reasoned that if the Freedom of Religion Clause forbids the government from telling people what to believe, it must also forbid the government from compelling people to express a belief different than their own. That means, at the very least, that the government may not *coerce* students to salute the flag by threatening them with expulsion from school and criminal prosecution. As the Court said:

> If there is any fixed star in our constitutional constellation, it is that no official, high or petty, can prescribe what shall be orthodox in politics, nationalism, religion, or other matters of opinion, or force citizens to confess by word or act their faith therein.[12]

As Justices Black and Douglas expressed in their concurring opinion in *Barnette*:

> Neither our domestic tranquility in peace nor our martial effort in war depend on compelling little children to participate in a ceremony which ends in nothing for them but a fear of spiritual condemnation. If, as we think, their fears are groundless, time and reason are the proper antidotes for their errors. The ceremonial, when enforced against conscientious objectors, …is a handy implement for disguised ***religious persecution***. As such, it is inconsistent with our Constitution's plan and purpose.[13] (Emphasis added.)

Wherein is the harm?

The result of the Court's ruling in *Barnette* is that public schools may make the Pledge of Allegiance and salute to the flag a part of their regular activities but they may not coerce students to participate in the activity by threatening them with expulsion from school or other punishment. School districts across the nation have lived with this rule, apparently without any major complaints or difficulties, for the past 60 years—and 50 years since the words "under God" were added in 1954. But Michael Newdow and the many people who support his position believe this is not enough. Newdow argues that even the voluntary recitation of the Pledge of Allegiance is unconstitutional because it, like school prayer, places the government's stamp of approval on a particular religious belief and coerces those present who do not join in that belief to be a participant in the activity going on around them. There are arguably two dangers that may arise from this situation. One is the subtle (and sometimes not-so-subtle) pressure placed on the school child to conform and join in the Pledge against his or her will. The second is the position the child finds himself in if he does not conform, that of being a dissenter and considered less patriotic—or less of an American—than his fellow classmates.

According to the Ninth Circuit, which agreed with Newdow, the current policy of leading only willing students in the Pledge of Allegiance:

> …places students in the untenable position of choosing between participating in an exercise with religious content or protesting…. The coercive effect of the policy here is particularly pronounced in the school setting given the age and impressionability of schoolchildren, and their understanding that they are required to adhere to the norms set by their school, their teacher and their fellow students…. The "subtle and indirect" social pressure which permeates the classroom also renders more acute the message sent to non-believing schoolchildren that they are outsiders….[14]

This too is a form of persecution. Anyone who doubts that people in this country might be persecuted for openly dissenting to the Pledge of Allegiance has only to ask Michael Newdow. The day after the Ninth Circuit ruled in his favor, he had an answering machine tape full of curses and threats from his fellow Americans and had city police officers making extra trips through his neighborhood to keep the peace. Although Newdow did much more than stand by in silent dissent while others recited the Pledge, the position he took clearly shows what can happen to those who choose not to conform.

The question then should be, are there sufficient reasons why school children should be required to participate in the Pledge of Allegiance, at least by listening respectfully while their teachers and fellow students recite it, even if this practice coerces some into saying the words of the Pledge without agreeing with it and leaves others to face the subtle persecution caused by open dissent? This is the primary question the Supreme Court will have to decide if, or rather when, it is faced with another challenge to the Pledge.

Wherein is the good?

The Pledge of Allegiance was originally written in 1892 by Francis Bellamy and published in a magazine titled *The Youth's Companion*. Bellamy wrote the pledge to be said as part of a celebration of the 400th anniversary of Christopher Columbus' arrival in the Americas.[15] The pledge became popular throughout the United States although it was not recognized at that time by any official act of the government. Around 1923, Bellamy's original words of "I pledge allegiance to my flag" were changed to "I pledge allegiance to the flag of the United States of America."[16] In June 1942, Congress added the Pledge of Allegiance to the United States Flag Code and included a description of the salute to be used when saying the Pledge: "extending the right hand, palm upward, toward the flag."[17] In December of the same year, the salute was changed from a straight arm, palm upward, salute (which resembled the Nazi salute to Hitler) to the currently-used salute of placing the right hand over the heart. Finally, in 1954, President Eisenhower approved the addition of the two words "under God" to the pledge.[18]

The words "under God" were added to the pledge during the Cold War to strengthen the concept of national unity and to remind Americans of the nature of our government. In the words of President Eisenhower:

These words will remind Americans that despite our great physical strength we must remain humble. They will help us to keep constantly in our minds and hearts the spiritual and moral principles which alone give dignity to man, and upon which our way of life is founded.[19]

And in the words of Representative Louis Rabault, who proposed the addition of the words "under God":

The most fundamental fact of this moment of history is that the principles of democratic government are being put to the test. The theory as to the nature of man which is the keystone in the arch of American Government is under attack by a system whose philosophy is exactly the opposite…. Our political institutions reflect the traditional American conviction of the worthwhileness of the individual human being. That conviction is, in turn, based on our belief that the human person is important because he has been created in the image and likeness of God and that he has been endowed by God with certain inalienable rights which no civil authority may usurp.[20]

A number of briefs filed in support of the Pledge of Allegiance support the same idea:

[T]he recitation of the Pledge with the phrase "under God"…encourages continuing recognition of the idea of God-given freedom—the very principle that unites Americans as a people.

Catholic League and Thomas More Law Center

The very notion that individuals arc endowed with basic unalienable human rights, gives meaning, life and substance to America's vision of self-governance…. If this source of our rights and liberties is not absolute in its existence then the very premise for our American vision is non-existent.

Common Good Foundation

The words of the Pledge echo the conviction held by the Founders of this Nation that our freedoms came from God. Congress inserted the phrase "one nation under God" in the Pledge of Allegiance for the express purpose of reaffirming America's unique understanding of this truth, and to distinguish America from atheistic nations who recognize no higher authority than the State.

Committee to Protect the Pledge and U.S. Senator Allen, et al.

The phrase was adopted to affirm the basis for this country's concept of limited government…. The reliance upon God as the source of inalienable individual rights is the most fundamental distinction between the political theory underlying our democratic republic and the Marxist-Leninist theory underlying the communist regime of the former Soviet Union.

Christian Legal Society, et al.

There it is—that old paradox again. The words "under God" were added to the Pledge of Allegiance to remind us of the principles upon which our nation was founded: that individuals have worth because they were created in the image of God, and that God gives certain rights to men the government cannot freely take away. These are religious principles, and when the government relies on these principles and requires that they be taught in public schools it is taking a position about the existence and nature of God. But our founding fathers also believed that every person is accountable to God alone for his moral choices and that it is no part of the government's business to tell people what to believe about God. Why not? Because of the two problems which have always existed when nations have tried to enforce uniform religious beliefs: the struggle between opposing groups to control or influence the government's religious agenda and the persecution of dissenters.

A Lesson from History

In June of 1940 when the Supreme Court rendered its decision in *Gobitis*, the nations of Europe were once again embroiled in a great war. Germany, still smarting from its losses in World War I, had occupied Czechoslovakia in March of 1939, and Italy had seized Albania the following month. When Germany invaded Poland in September 1939, France and Britain entered the war to protect their ally.[21] The Second World War had begun, and the United States was determined to stay out of it.

Two months before *Gobitis* was decided, Denmark fell to German forces. Norway fell next, six days after the Court's decision. On June 22, 1940, France signed an armistice with Germany leaving the government of France in Nazi hands. Hungary, Romania, and Bulgaria joined the Axis powers of Germany and Italy which then defeated Yugoslavia, Greece, and Crete. Germany bombarded England by air while Italy launched attacks against British holdings in Africa, and far across the continent of Asia, Japan moved against European holdings in Burma, the East Indies, and Singapore. On December 7, 1941, Japan attacked Pearl Harbor. Germany and Italy, allied with Japan, declared war against the United States a few days later.[22]

In the spring of 1943, when the Supreme Court sat down to consider the *Barnette* case, the United States was deeply involved in the war. The Pledge of Allegiance had been added to the Flag Code the previous year, undoubtedly to promote national pride, national unity, and (as the Court noted in *Gobitis*) national security. The pledge highlighted the differences between the fascist regimes of Germany and Italy and the democratic principles of America. It reminded us of the ideals of "liberty and justice for all," which stood in stark contrast to Hitler's belief in the supremacy of the Aryan race and the right of the strong to conquer the weak. However, there was one area in which the United States was in danger of becoming like the enemy. Like the people of Germany, the citizens of this country found strength in unity. Hitler promoted unity through national pride and the silencing of dissent. He appealed to the masses with passion and fanaticism, with propaganda rather than with truth. He once wrote: "All effective propaganda has to limit itself to a very few points and to use them like slogans…. It has to confine itself to little and to repeat this eternally."[23] Perhaps this is what the Court was thinking about when it wrote the following:

Struggles to coerce uniformity of sentiment in support of some end thought essential to their time and country have been waged by many good as well as by evil men…. As governmental pressure toward unity becomes greater, so strife becomes more bitter as to whose unity it shall be. Probably no deeper division of our people could proceed from any provocation than from finding it necessary to choose what doctrine and whose program public educational officials shall compel youth to unite in embracing. Ultimate futility of such attempts to compel coherence is the lesson of every such effort from the Roman drive to stamp out Christianity as a disturber of its pagan unity, the Inquisition, as a means to religious and dynastic unity, the Siberian exiles as a means to Russian unity, down to the fast failing efforts of our present totalitarian enemies. Those who begin coercive elimination of dissent soon find themselves exterminating dissenters. Compulsory unification of opinion achieves only the unanimity of the graveyard.[24]

Chapter 5

The Third Option

Choose for yourselves this day whom you will serve,
whether the gods your forefathers served beyond the River,
or the gods of the Amorites, in whose land you are living.
But as for me and my household, we will serve the Lord.
~ Joshua 24:15 ~

Out of curiosity, I checked a thesaurus to see what synonyms I could find for the word "paradox." It listed "inconsistency," "absurdity," "contradiction in terms," "impossibility," "irony," and "illogicality." It left out one of my favorite words: "oxymoronic," which means "a combination of contradictory or incongruous words…or something that is made up of contradictory or incongruous elements."[1] It might also have included the old colloquialism, "you can't have your cake and eat it too" (which never made much sense to me, since the whole point of having a piece of cake is to eat it). The point of all these words and phrases is that you can't have things two ways. You have to choose. If you don't choose, the choice might be made for you.

Our founding fathers and the framers of the Constitution could not choose. They felt our nation needed God's protection and guidance for it to have any chance of survival, but they deeply feared taking an official position with regards to who God is and what his desire is for his people. They had good reasons for both of these beliefs. In the end, they compromised. On one hand, they chose to guarantee religious liberty and to protect that liberty by preventing the government from establishing or supporting any religion or any particular religious belief. On the other hand, they continued to encourage religious belief by calling on God for support and thanking him for his blessings in a variety of official actions. Because of their inability to choose, some might say the United States has been left without the moral guidance it needs and has steadily declined in decency and integrity ever since. Others argue that our governments (both state and federal) have been handicapped by religion, leading to narrow-minded policies and intolerance.

An obvious solution to the problem is, of course, to choose. The United States can either become the Christian nation so many believe it can be, the "city upon a hill" that some of the early settlers hoped to establish under God's guidance and blessing,[2] or the government can finally finish that wall of separation and truly make religion no part of the government's business. Most Christians immediately balk at that second idea. In fact, most Americans do not like the idea, as shown by the 90% approval rating of leaving the words "under God" in the Pledge of Allegiance. But the idea of truly being a "Christian" nation at least arguably denies to the many who do not believe in Jesus Christ an equal place in our society and leads to intolerance and persecution.

The question then arises, is there another choice? Can our nation find a way to publicly acknowledge God and the role of religion in our national heritage without being intolerant of other faiths, or even the lack of faith, and can we do that consistently with the Establishment Clause of the First Amendment?

A Secular Purpose

Over the years, the Supreme Court has established a test to determine if an action of the government complies with the Establishment Clause. To pass this test the government's action must have a secular (non-religious) purpose; it must not be intended to advance or inhibit religion; and it must not result in excessive involvement by the government in religious matters.[3] In a number of cases, the Court has used this test to find that actions of the government which appear "religious" on their face do not violate the Establishment Clause because the true purpose of the government's action was secular, rather than religious, in nature. Two such cases were mentioned in Chapter Three. In one, the Court ruled that a city government could place a nativity scene beside a Santa Clause house in a shopping district because the display had a commercial rather than a religious purpose,[4] and in the second, a county government could place a menorah and Christmas tree together in a public square because the combined display recognized the cultural traditions of the holiday season rather than specific religious beliefs.[5]

Justice O'Connor has perhaps explained this middle ground position better than anyone else:

> Although the religious and indeed sectarian significance of [these religious symbols] is not neutralized by the setting, the overall holiday setting changes what viewers may fairly understand to be the purpose of the display—as a typical museum setting, though not neutralizing the religious content of a religious painting, negates any message of endorsement of that content. The display celebrates a public holiday, and no one contends that declaration of that holiday is understood to be an endorsement of religion. The holiday itself has very strong secular components and traditions.[6]

In other words, just like a museum may display a religious painting without endorsing the beliefs depicted in the painting, the government may display religious symbols in certain settings that emphasize the cultural and traditional elements of the symbols rather than their religious meanings.

Justice O'Connor went on to say that the religious display in question in that case was:

> no more an endorsement of religion than such governmental "acknowledgements" of religion as legislative prayers…, government declaration of Thanksgiving as a public holiday, printing of "In God We Trust" on coins, and opening court sessions with "God save the United States and this honorable court." Those governmental acknowledgments of religion serve, in the only ways reasonably possible in our culture, the legitimate secular purposes of solemnizing public occasions, expressing confidence in the future, and encouraging the recognition of what is worthy of appreciation in society. For that reason, and because of their history and ubiquity, those practices are not understood as conveying government approval of particular religious beliefs.[7]

This idea of using religious symbols and phrases for secular purposes was given further approval in the same opinion by Justice Brennan:

> [S]uch practices as the designation of "In God We Trust" as our national motto, or the references to God contained in the Pledge of Allegiance to the flag can best be understood… as a form a "ceremonial deism," protected from Establishment Clause scrutiny chiefly because they have lost through rote repetition any significant religious content. Moreover, these references are uniquely suited to serve such wholly secular purposes as solemnizing public occasions, or inspiring commitment to meet some national challenge in a manner that simply could not be fully served in our culture if government were limited to purely nonreligious phrases.[8]

If you were not struck by something very disturbing in the last three quotes, go back and read them again. They are suggesting that the proper and only way our government can acknowledge religion in America is to *use* it. Religious symbols and expressions are all right if they are used in such a way as to *serve* the purposes of the government in "solemnizing public occasions," "inspiring commitment," and even encouraging Christmas shopping. They are not all right if they are perceived to suggest that the leaders of our government actually believe in God and have any responsibility to him.

This idea of "ceremonial deism" is now being used as an argument to support the Pledge of Allegiance. According to the government's petition to the Supreme Court to review the pledge case:

> [T]he addition of the phrase "under God" to the Pledge was done for a secular purpose—the affirmation of the concept that the United States was founded on a fundamental belief in God. The phrase does not compel anyone to believe in the existence of God or recognize religion in general. Instead, it merely reflects the role of religion in the history of the United States.[9]

What we honor in the pledge, according to this argument, is not God, but the religious beliefs of those who founded this nation, whether those beliefs were right or wrong. This is the position urged by the majority of the *amicus* briefs that were filed in the Supreme Court in support of the Pledge of Allegiance and the one most likely to be accepted by the Court if the Court eventually rules in favor of the constitutionality of the pledge.

The God of our Fathers

If nothing else, it is an interesting argument. It admits that our nation was founded upon a fundamental belief in God, but says it is the *belief* in God by the majority of the people, rather than the *truth* of God's existence and authority, that is the important factor.

Among the uses of religion given above, others have been suggested throughout our history: that people who believe in a righteous God are more likely to be virtuous and law abiding; that people who believe in a loving God are more likely to care for their neighbors and their country; and that our system of government is preferable to any other because it is based on godly principles. The people's *belief* in God then forms the foundation for good citizenship and a lasting republic, rather than God himself supporting and blessing our nation.

Is this heresy? Is this treason? Does this go against everything our founding fathers believed? Has the Supreme Court completely abandoned the God of our fathers in favor of a superficial religion the only purpose of which is to keep the masses obedient to the government?

Consider the following quotes from some of the founding fathers.[10] But read them very carefully. Ask yourself if the speaker is more concerned with the *truth* of religious beliefs or the *usefulness* of them.

> Of all the dispositions and habits which lead to political prosperity, Religion and morality are indispensable supports. In vain would that man claim the tribute of Patriotism, who should labor to subvert these great Pillars of human happiness, these firmest props of the duties of Men and citizens.
>
> *George Washington*

> We have no government armed with powers capable of contending with human passions unbridled by morality and religion.
>
> *John Adams*

> Only a virtuous people are capable of freedom.
>
> *Benjamin Franklin*

Can the liberties of a nation be thought secure when we have removed their only firm basis, a conviction in the minds of the people, that these liberties are the gift of God? that they are violated but with his wrath?

Thomas Jefferson

The belief in a God All Powerful, wise, and good, is so essential to the moral order of the World and to the happiness of man, that arguments which enforce it cannot be drawn from too many sources nor adapted with too much solicitude to the different characters impressed with it.

James Madison

No human society has ever been able to maintain both order and freedom, both cohesiveness and liberty apart from the moral precepts of the Christian Religion applied and accepted by all the classes. Should our Republic ever forget this fundament precept of governance, men are certain to shed their responsibilities for licentiousness and this great experiment will then surely be doomed.

John Jay

If, as we have seen…, virtue and piety are inseparably connected, then to promote true religion is the best and most effectual way of making a virtuous and regular people. Love to God, and love to man, is the substance of religion; when these prevail, civil laws will have little to do.

John Witherspoon

My purpose here is not to suggest that all of the founding fathers were religious hypocrites who only professed to believe in God for their own objectives. Many other quotes could be given to show that each of these men believed in a God who created the world and ordained rules of basic morality. What I want to point out is that using a belief in God as a tool to promote good citizenship and a lasting government is not a new idea concocted by a few Justices on the Supreme Court. It is an idea which has been around since the founding of our country—and long before that. It is the same idea which was used to support the rule of monarchs, emperors, and pharaohs ever since nations began. Whether you believe that God grants the power to rule to a king or to the people, that belief compels you to submit to the authority which is granted or to suffer eternal consequences.

The idea of "ceremonial deism"—using the superficial trappings of religion to support the authority of the government—strikes some as heresy, bordering on idolatry. For the atheist it may simply seem illogical. But for many people in the modern society of America, the idea presents a comfortable compromise between the moral demands of fundamental Christianity and the emptiness of atheism. It allows our government to encourage virtue and morality through religion, but leaves each person free to choose the brand of religion or spiritual experience which suits them best. We can all feel better believing there is a God, believing he will protect us, and believing that our form of government is good in his sight, without seriously considering whether any of these things are true or not.

A Religion of Compromise

It was said by one of the greatest legal minds of our nation that "the men who met in 1787 to make a Constitution made the best political document ever made, [and] they did it very largely because they were great compromisers."[11] They compromised to create a balance of power between the state and federal governments. They compromised to provide fair representation of larger and smaller states. They compromised on the issue of slavery, foregoing the chance to end an institution considered by so many to be opposed to the ideals of liberty and equality for which the colonies had just fought. And they compromised on religion.

Two religious ideals struggled for supremacy during our nation's formative years. One was the ideal of the Puritans who fled to the shores of New England to escape what they saw as the false religion of the Anglican Church. They undertook their voyage to the New World "for the Glory of God, and advancement of the Christian Faith,"[12] and wanted to form a community of believers which would be a "city upon a hill."[13] As the first governor of the Massachusetts Bay Colony, John Winthrop, wrote in 1630:

> [T]he Lord will be our God and delight to dwell among us as his own people and will command a blessing upon us in all our ways, so that we shall see much more of his wisdom, power, goodness and truth then formerly we have been acquainted with; we shall find that the God of Israel is among us, when ten of us shall be able to resist a thousand of our enemies, when he shall make us a praise and glory, that men shall say of succeeding [colonies]: the Lord make it like that of New England....[14]

The second ideal was that of the Age of Enlightenment which stressed individual freedom and the responsibility of the individual to worship God according to the dictates of his own conscience. To the "enlightened" thinker, God's salvation could not be imposed by society, and the government should have no say at all on questions of religion. James Madison summed this idea up nicely:

> [W]e hold it for a fundamental and undeniable truth, "that religion, or the duty which we owe to our Creator, and the manner of discharging it, can be directed only by reason and conviction, not by force or violence." The Religion then of every man must be left to the conviction and conscience of every man; and it is the right of every man to exercise it as these may

dictate…. It is the duty of every man to render to the Creator such homage, and such only, as he believes to be acceptable to him.[15]

By the time the Constitution was being written, many of the founding fathers agreed with the idea of the Puritans that some unity of religious thought and moral guidance was needed as a foundation for their new nation, but they could not ignore the arguments of the Enlightenment that religious uniformity enforced by the government invariably leads to division and persecution. Members of different faiths in the new states could find little on which to agree. The minority of Catholics considered their Protestant neighbors as unrepentant heretics. The Protestants thought of Catholics as idolaters. The growing number of Unitarians and deists believed in the existence of God based on rational arguments, but they rejected the divinity of Jesus Christ and the authority of the Bible. The only way to find a unity of religious belief was to reduce each group's doctrine to the lowest common denominator, which was little more than the belief in a supernatural being who created the world and will someday judge it.

Rather than risk the unity of the nation over a search for a unity of religious doctrine, the founders accepted one another's right to believe what they would, as long as those beliefs did not conflict with the person's civic duties or infringe on anyone else's right to believe. Had they stopped there, the world indeed may have learned the lesson James Madison hoped it would, "that religion flourishes in greater purity without, than with the aid of government."[16] But the leaders of our nation, from the very beginning, went further. They continued to place an emphasis on religion and God as part of our national identity, invoking the name of God in speeches, in formal oaths, on public buildings, on coins, and in the daily pledge to the flag. But as the diversity of religious beliefs in the United States has grown, the common ground of religious identity has been stretched almost to the point of being nonexistent. What we have left is a nameless, faceless, generic "God"—a "God" of many definitions and choices—a "God" whose only power is to solemnize occasions, inspire commitment, and set us apart from "godless" nations.

Add to the mix of religious beliefs in this country the anti-religious teachings of evolution and humanism, and the "God" of our nation has almost no substance at all. The same school children who are encouraged by the Pledge of Allegiance to remember the fundamental religious beliefs of their forefathers are taught from kindergarten on that man was *not* created in the image of God, but that we evolved over billions of years from pond scum! These children must wonder who the "God" is that our nation is "under" and why the president asks us once a year to pray to him.

When we truly look at America and our public acknowledgements of God, we find there is little more to it than ceremonial trappings. It is a compromise that, for the most part, we are comfortable with. We can claim God's guidance for our nation, ask for his blessing, and call ourselves "godly" because we live in a nation that "believes" in God. This is the third option, the compromise between a single, true religion and no religion at all. We keep our public references to God and the trappings of our Christian heritage but remove from them any real meaning. We give honor to God in a form of religious observance with no substance. We practice a one-size-fits-all religion which calls on a "God" who is tolerant of all beliefs, there when you need him, and always forgiving. But does such a God even exist?

Whom Will You Serve?

The Bible spends a great amount of time talking about false gods. The first commandment charges us to have no other gods before the one true God (Exodus 20:2-3). The second commandment warns us not to create idols or to bow down and serve them (Exodus 20:4-5). Exodus 20:23 says, "Do not make any gods to be alongside me; do not make for yourselves gods of silver or gods of gold." But at the very time Moses was on top of Mount Sinai receiving these commandments from the true God of Israel, the Children of Israel were at the bottom of the mountain commanding Moses' brother Aaron to make them another god—a god of gold—to go before them. Aaron took their gold earrings, melted them down, and fashioned a calf for the people to worship. The people danced and partied before the calf until Moses came down from the mountain, still physically glowing from being in the presence of the one true God. In his disgust, Moses ground the golden calf into powder, threw it in the water, and made the Israelites drink it. The gold the Israelites had plundered from the Egyptians at God's command—the prosperity God had blessed them with as they left the bonds of slavery and set off to the Promised Land—was taken away and left behind in the desert along with their bodily refuse (Exodus 12:33-36; 32:1-20).

It is not only false gods that God detests, he also detests false worship. The third commandment tells us not to take God's name in vain, not to misuse it or to use it in a frivolous or meaningless way (Exodus 20:7). How often did God say through the Old Testament prophets that he wanted much more than empty acts of worship? "To obey is better than sacrifice, and to heed is better than the fat of rams" (1 Samuel 15:22). "For I desire mercy, not sacrifice, and acknowledgment of God rather than burnt offerings" (Hosea 6:6). "I hate, I despise your religious feasts; I cannot stand your assemblies.... Away with the noise of your songs! I will not listen to the music of your harps. But let justice roll on like a river, righteousness like a never-failing stream!" (Amos 5:21, 23-24). "These people...honor me with their lips, but their hearts are far from me. Their worship of me is made up only of rules taught by men" (Isaiah 29:13). Jesus also warned against empty worship, calling the Jewish religious leaders of his day hypocrites who had "let go of the commands of God and are holding on to the traditions of men" (Mark 7:8).

God is not pleased by empty words unaccompanied by true commitment and obedience. He is not impressed by having his name written on buildings and on coins and recited on a daily basis in school buildings by children who have no real knowledge of him. He is not satisfied with being one choice among many recognized by our schools and our government in the new spirit of "multiculturalism." He hates it! He refuses to listen to the "noise" of our songs, our oaths, our pledges, and our prayers. He is offended, and rightfully so, by the multitude of people who call themselves "spiritual" or "godly" or even "Christians," who acknowledge God's existence but who will not listen to his word. And when we, as true Christians, join in this hypocrisy—and even encourage it—we offend him, too.

Chapter 6

Blessed is the Nation

Blessed is the man who always fears the Lord,
but he who hardens his heart falls into trouble.
~ Proverbs 28:14 ~

There are undoubtedly instances in which compromise is a good thing. The whole world of politics is about making compromises between the many groups who are represented by the politicians. One group gets part of what it wants and another group gets part of what it wants. In a nation as diverse as ours has become—both culturally and in political ideology—the inability to compromise often results in an inability to do anything. But in the area of religion, which I will define here as that duty of worship and obedience we owe to our Creator, there is no room for compromise. What *we* want really doesn't matter. God's kingdom is not a democracy, but a theocracy. He alone is in charge.

Empty religious ceremonies without obedience to God are worthless. They are worse than worthless. God detests them. We should not say we are a religious nation, or a "Christian" nation, or a nation "under God" without actually living in obedience to God. So, for many people it would seem there is only one choice left: To truly become a Christian nation. There are groups in America trying to make this happen. Using their rights to petition the government, to communicate their ideas through the media, and to try to persuade others to agree with and support their values, these groups seek legislation and public policy in line with traditional moral, Christian values. They speak out on issues such as abortion, education, marriage, parenting, and religious freedom. They believe our nation should return to the ideals of the founding fathers who, although they did not all ascribe to the same religious beliefs, all shared the same commitment of moral responsibility to a supreme being.

A number of years ago, I was encouraged to join such a group in my home state and to use my legal training to aid their cause. I spoke to a number of people about the group, all of whom were very supportive of the idea of bringing Christian values back to America. One of the reasons they support this idea is their belief that an America based on Christian values would be a nicer, safer, more comfortable place to live. No murder, no theft, no adultery, no lying. Respect for others, respect for property, respect for the government and its laws. Respect for life. Respect for marriage and family. Public schools that teach abstinence until marriage and don't try to convince our kids that they evolved from monkeys. Freedom to pray in school.

Wouldn't it be nice to live in a nation where you don't have to worry about what your children will learn in school, whether they will be safe there, and whether you can turn on your car radio without being swamped with foul language and even fouler ideas? Wouldn't it be easier if our government supported the same values we choose for ourselves and forbid behavior that goes against those values? If the Bible says homosexuality, abortion, and pagan religions are sinful, why not have laws against them? Let the government make people behave themselves. Isn't that its job?

But I didn't join the group. I debated the pros and cons of supporting Christian values through legislation. I cried and prayed through September 11, 2001, wondering if this tragedy would have happened if America had not forsaken its earlier values. I wondered what Christians should do to encourage righteous living in this country. Then I asked the bigger question: Should we even try? Is that really what God wants us to do? Or are we more concerned with what *we* want than what God wants? After reading the last few chapters, if you are still holding fast to your desire to say the Pledge of Allegiance with the words "under God" in it and listen to your president talk about God's will for America and see your representatives pass laws against same-sex marriage and abortion and obscenity, ask yourself this: What is your motivation? Could it possibly be one of the following?

Motivation #1: Comfort

Perhaps you are like the people I talked to in my church. You are uncomfortable living in a nation where so many people do not hold the same values you do. You don't like seeing two people of the same sex holding hands and kissing. You disapprove of the immodest clothes teenagers (and many adults) wear. You wish there was less violence, less vulgarity, and less sex on television and at the movies. You are trying hard to raise your children or grandchildren with good manners and good morals in a society which increasingly tells them to make their own rules.

If any of these descriptions applies to you, you are certainly not alone. I'm right in there with you. It's not easy to carry on a constant battle against the world to keep our minds and hearts—and those of our children—pure. But that is what God asks us to do. Jesus told his disciples, "Watch and pray so that you will not fall into temptation" (Matthew 26:41). The apostle Paul told the elders of Ephesus:

> Keep watch over yourselves and all the flock of which the Holy Spirit has made you overseers…. I know that after I leave, savage wolves will come in among you and will not spare the flock. Even from your own number men will arise and distort the truth in order to draw away disciples after them. So be on your guard! (Acts 20:28-30)

We are told to be on our guard against the temptations of the world because those temptations will always be there. God does not want you to get comfortable in your own little part of the world. He wants you to be constantly on guard against the forces of evil around you. Nor does God want you to "fit in" in an ungodly world. The apostle Paul writes:

> Do not be yoked together with unbelievers. For what do righteousness and wickedness have in common? Or what fellowship can light have with darkness? ... What does a believer have in common with an unbeliever? ... Therefore come out from them and be separate, says the Lord. (2 Corinthians 6:14-17)

This does not mean to say that we should pack our bags, like the Pilgrims of old, and move to a new world to escape the evils of our present world. God does not tell us to have nothing to do with the people of the world. He tells us to have nothing to do with the way they live. He tells us to be different. To look different to other people. To think and act in a different way because we have the revealed Word of God and the power of the Holy Spirit. A lamp is not needed in a room already full of light. God calls us to be a light to a darkened world. One important thing to remember about a lamp in a dark room is that it stands out. It is different. Being different isn't comfortable, but it is God's command.

> You are the light of the world. A city on a hill cannot be hidden. Neither do people light a lamp and put it under a bowl. Instead they put it on its stand, and it gives light to everyone in the house. In the same way, let your light shine before men, that they may see your good deeds and praise your Father in heaven. (Matthew 5:14-16)

Trying to change the laws and policies of America for our own comfort is not God's will. If we are going to be a "Christian" nation, it should not be because it makes life a little easier for those of us who are Christians.

Motivation #2: Fear

But if we do not try to change our ways and become more moral as a nation, won't God punish us? Is not the God of the Bible a God of justice and mighty wrath? How many great cities in the Old Testament suffered from God's righteous fury? Nineveh, Tyre and Sidon, Sodom and Gomorrah. The prophets sent out warnings to the nations of Edom, Philistia, Moab, Ammon, and Cush about God's impending judgment. They warned Israel and Judah also.

When the children of Israel did not obey God he sent them into captivity in Assyria and Babylon. After seventy years of captivity, the kingdom of Judah was restored for a time, but in the year 70 A.D., Jerusalem was destroyed again and the nation of Israel ceased to exist for almost two millennia. By that time, all the books of the Bible had been written, the Christian church had been established and was growing, and a New Covenant had been offered by God to both the Jew and the Gentile. But God's judgment did not stop there. He did not finish his work and then take his hands off of the world to let the nations do as they would. His work was not yet completed, and it still isn't. Many of the prophecies of the Old and New Testaments have yet to be fulfilled, and many of those prophecies deal with judgment against ungodly nations.

> Come near, you nations, and listen; pay attention, you peoples! Let the earth hear, and all that is in it, the world, and all that comes out of it! The Lord is angry with all nations; his wrath is upon all their armies. He will totally destroy them, he will give them over to slaughter. (Isaiah 34:1-2)

The Bible tells us very clearly that God will judge the nations. So it is only natural we should be afraid for our own nation. But we have to be careful about what that fear motivates us to do. For the most part, people who want America to be more obedient to God want this because of what they, themselves, have to lose. We think that if America ever degrades morally so far as to get God really angry, God is likely to pour out his wrath on us. We might be conquered by another nation, weakened by natural disasters or diseases, or destroyed by our own mistreatment of the environment or scientific advances. Everything we have here we could lose, including our security, our freedom, and our material possessions. Isn't that a good reason to try to change America? Shouldn't we try to make laws which are pleasing to God so he will not take away the things we treasure?

If this is your fear, then consider the words of Jesus:

> Do not store up for yourselves treasures on earth, where moth and rust destroy, and where thieves break in and steal. But store up for yourselves treasures in heaven, where moth and rust do not destroy, and where thieves do not break in and steal. For where your treasure is, there your heart will be also. (Matthew 6:19-21)

Jesus compared the kingdom of heaven to a pearl of great price that would cause someone to be willing to sell everything he or she had in order to possess it (Matthew 13:44-46). He told the story of a rich fool who spent all his time building storehouses for his goods on earth, only to die without enjoying them (Luke 12:16-21). He advised a wealthy young man to sell all he had and give to the poor to gain a treasure in heaven (Mark 10:17-27). He encouraged us not to worry about what we will eat or what we will wear, but to seek first the kingdom of God "and all these things will be given to you as well" (Matthew 6:25-33). Jesus did not want us to be afraid of what we might lose on this earth. He wanted us to give up *everything* for him.

> If anyone would come after me, he must deny himself and take up his cross and follow me. For whoever wants to save his life will lose it, but whoever loses his life for me and for the gospel will save it. What good is it for a man to gain the whole world, yet forfeit his soul? (Mark 8:34-36)

What *we* stand to lose should not be a motivating factor in our decision about what is best for America. We'll have to come up with something better than that.

Motivation #3: Concern for Others

What about non-Christians, then? Shouldn't we be concerned for our friends and family and neighbors who have not accepted God's saving grace? If America is destroyed, won't they be destroyed with it? If we can put off God's wrath by living according to his law, shouldn't we encourage moral behavior among unbelievers for their own good?

These are all valid questions, but they are focused in the wrong direction. Someday everyone is going to die.

> Just as man is destined to die once, and after that to face judgment, so Christ was sacrificed once to take away the sins of many people; and he will appear a second time, not to bear sin, but to bring salvation to those who are waiting for him. (Hebrews 9:27-28)

Jesus did not come into the world to save people's lives and stop us from dying. He came to save our souls. He came to offer himself as a sacrifice to pay the penalty for our sins so we might be reconciled to God and live with him forever. People aren't saved because they are good or because they obey the law, even God's law, because no one can perfectly obey that law.

> But God demonstrates his own love for us in this: While we were still sinners, Christ died for us. Since we have now been justified by his blood, how much more shall we be saved from God's wrath through him. For if, when we were God's enemies, we were reconciled to him through the death of his Son, how much more, having been reconciled, shall we be saved through his life! (Romans 5:8-10)

It is not obedience or goodness or outward displays of worship that reconcile us to God. It is only Jesus. It is he who said, "I am the way and the truth and the life. No one comes to the Father except through me" (John 14:6). The only people who ever really get that, though, are the ones who recognize they are sinners—that they are not worthy of

God's love or mercy. The comfortable, the prosperous, the respected, the "good" people of our world are often the hardest to reach with the good news of the gospel because they do not see their need of it. This is what Jesus meant when he said, "I have not come to call the righteous, but sinners" (Matthew 9:13). He did not mean there were some people who were obedient to God and did not need him. He meant there were some people who were righteous in their own eyes and would never accept him. Those same self-righteous "teachers of the law" he later called hypocrites, whitewashed tombs, blind fools, and snakes (Matthew 23). Jesus had no time for those who outwardly obeyed the law but had no real love for God or for man. Jesus went to the humble, the weak, the social outcasts, and the law-breakers and offered them God's forgiveness and love.

Laws do not save people. Good acts do not save people, nor do good intentions. Only Jesus saves. "Through him and for his name's sake, we received grace and apostleship to call people from among all the Gentiles to the *obedience that comes from faith*" (Romans 1:5). It is only through faith in Jesus that we will ever be able to live a life pleasing to God. So our efforts would be better focused on saving individuals from the penalty of sin than in trying to save a nation from the eventual judgement of God.

Motivation #4: Freedom

Another reason we might want to make America a more "Christian" nation is to keep the blessings God has given us, including the freedom to worship him and to speak freely. If we were ever to lose those freedoms, we believe we would also lose the ability to teach others about God and his plan of salvation because our freedoms allow us to spread the gospel throughout our own nation and the world. If our nation is obedient to God he will continue to bless us with freedom, and we can use our resources for God's glory. We can win people to Christ, in this country and in others, by our nation's example of righteous living. Can't we?

Perhaps the question should be, *do* we? It is nice having the freedom to attend church openly and to join Christian organizations, but when is the last time you used your freedom of speech to tell someone else about Jesus? How much of your resources (time, money and talent) are you investing each week in spreading the gospel of Christ? Is the church you freely go to encouraging you to study and grow in God's Word, or is it just a nice place to meet with people who share your values and traditions? In other words, are you using your freedoms for God's glory or for your own comfort?

It would be nice, of course, if all Christians in America truly used the freedoms and resources with which we are blessed to do God's work in the world. But even if we did, would that be enough of a reason to force non-Christians in this country to live by our rules? It might put off God's day of wrath and keep America secure. But should we assume that we can do God's work better with the gifts of freedom and prosperity than without them? God's Word would seem to indicate that the opposite is true.

The book of Acts takes up the story of the disciples and apostles after the resurrection and ascension of Jesus. On the day of Pentecost, Peter preached the good news of the gospel to a large crowd of people in Jerusalem "and about three thousand people were added to their number" (Acts 2:41). Had Peter been living in the United States, that might have been the end of the story, but he lived in Israel in the first century, where freedom of speech had never been heard of. Shortly after Pentecost, Peter and his friend John were arrested for preaching outside the temple. "They seized Peter and John, and because it was evening, they put them in jail until the next day. *But many who heard the message believed*, and the number of men grew to about five thousand" (Acts 4:3-4).

After their release from jail, Peter and John continued to spread the gospel, ignoring the threats and warnings of their nation's religious leaders. New disciples sold their belongings and shared all they had with one another. When one couple lied about the amount they had received for selling some property, God struck them dead in punishment, and "*more men and women believed and were added to their number*" (Acts 5:14). Stephen was stoned to death for telling people about Jesus. Believers were persecuted in Jerusalem and many were forced to leave the city. But *"those who had been scattered preached the word wherever they went"* (Acts 8:4). Peter was arrested again and set free by an angel. James, the brother of John, was executed. Paul was accused, beaten, and chased out of almost every city that he ever visited. And still the Church grew!

> You, however, know all about my teaching, my way of life, my purpose, faith, patience, love, endurance, persecutions, sufferings—what kinds of things happened to me in Antioch, Iconium and Lystra, the persecutions I endured. Yet the Lord rescued me from all of them…. The Lord stood at my side and gave me strength, so that through me the message might be fully proclaimed and all the Gentiles might hear it. And I was delivered from the lion's mouth. (2 Timothy 3:10-11, 4:17)

Paul's testimony should make one thing perfectly clear. God is able to overcome any obstacle in the furtherance of his work. You don't need to be free to worship God. You don't need to feel secure to tell others about Jesus Christ. The Gospel of Christ is spreading all around the world right now, in communist countries, in Muslim countries, in places where God's people face imprisonment, beatings, loss of jobs or property, and even death. Freedom of religion, freedom of speech, peace and prosperity—none of these are necessary to the work of God. They may even be a hindrance, if we come to love these freedoms more than we love God.

> Do not love the world or anything in the world. If anyone loves the world, the love of the Father is not in him. For everything in the world—the cravings of sinful man, the lust of his eyes and the boasting of what he has and does— comes not from the Father but from the world. The world and its desires pass away, but the man who does the will of God lives forever. (1 John 2:15-17)

Motivation #5: Pride

But God did give us those freedoms, didn't he? He has blessed us and given us a special role in the world, hasn't he? Isn't that why we all say so proudly, "God Bless America"? You see it everywhere—on billboards and bumper-stickers, on church message boards and political buttons. Some people say it as a prayer, but more and more it seems to be said as a boast. "God Bless the Good Guys." That's us! American pride is more prevalent than the love of baseball and hotdogs and shopping at the mall. It is the one thing that ties all Americans together. We love our country, and we're proud of it. We want God to be proud of it, too. And we want all the nations of the earth to know how special we are. We always have, from the foundation of our nation to today:

> I always consider the settlement of America with reverence and wonder, as the opening of a grand scene and design in Providence for the illumination of the ignorant, and the emancipation of the slavish part of mankind all over the earth.
>
> *John Adams, 1765*[1]

> [God] has marked the American people as His chosen nation to finally lead in the regeneration of the world. This is the divine mission of America, and it holds for us all the profit, all the glory, all the happiness possible to man. We are trustees of the world's progress, guardians of its righteous peace.
>
> *U.S. Senator Albert J. Beveridge, 1900*[2]

> He believed people were basically good, and had the right to be free. He believed in the Golden Rule and the power of prayer. He believed America wasn't just a place in the world, but the hope of the world.
>
> *President George W. Bush, in eulogy of Ronald Reagan, 2004*[3]

The idea that the United States of America has been chosen by God for a special purpose in the world has been with us since our beginning. The next chapter will explore that idea in some detail. But even if this assumption is correct, why would we think that God chose America for *our* profit, *our* glory, and *our* happiness, as Senator Beveridge stated a century ago? Would it not be for *his* glory? If pride in our country is one of our motivating factors in pushing for a more moral society, we would do well to consider the following warnings:

> Pride goes before destruction, a haughty spirit before a fall. (Proverbs 16:18)

> Do not think of yourself more highly than you ought, but rather think of yourself with sober judgment, in accordance with the measure of faith God has given you. (Romans 12:3)

Sober judgment is what America needs most at this moment in history, not pride. If we are indeed a chosen people, then let God do his work through us for his glory. Let us not be like the Pharisees of Jesus' day. Although they knew for a fact that God had chosen their nation for a special purpose, they were so certain they understood God's plan that they completely missed what God was doing in their midst. Being mindful of their example, we should be very careful to not get so caught up in what we *think* God will do through us that we miss the wonderful and marvelous things he *is* doing.

> "Let not the wise man boast of his wisdom or the strong man boast of his strength or the rich man boast of his riches, but let him who boasts boast about this: that he understands and knows me, that I am the Lord, who exercises kindness, justice and righteousness on earth, for in these I delight," declares the Lord. (Jeremiah 9:23-24)

Chapter 7

A Chosen People

I will make you into a great nation and I will bless you; I will make your name
great, and you will be a blessing. I will bless those who bless you, and whoever
curses you I will curse; and all people on earth will be blessed through you.
~ Genesis 12:2-3 ~

Should we be striving to make the United States a moral "Christian" nation, a nation pleasing to God and a blessing to the earth? If we are doing it for our own pride, or comfort, or out of fear of what we might lose, the answer is no, we shouldn't. Should we do it for God's glory, then? That depends on whether it is God's will that we do so. You see, no matter how much we try to please God by what we do, all he really *wants* us to do is what he has *asked* us to do. God has a plan for the world. He is in control. If you are at all confused about what God's plan is for you or for our nation, all you have to do is go back to his Word and see what it tells you. No, God doesn't talk about America in the Bible. But he does talk about his plan for the whole world. He wants us to get in line with that plan and to let him work things out his way—not ours.

A Nation and a Promise

"I will make you into a great nation." Those words were spoken by God to Abram, a man living 4000 years ago in the city of Ur by the Euphrates River. By faith, Abram left his home and traveled to a distant land, taking with him his wife, his nephew, and all his possessions. In this new land, God gave Abram the name of Abraham—father of many— and told him his descendants would be as numerous as the stars in the sky and God would give them the whole land around him as "an everlasting possession" (Genesis 12:1-5, 15:5, 17: 3-8). God repeated this promise to Abraham's grandson, Jacob—whom he renamed Israel:

> I will give you and your descendants the land on which you are lying. Your descendants will be like the dust of the earth, and you will spread out to the west and to the east, to the north and to the south. All peoples on earth will be blessed through you and your offspring. I am with you and will watch over you wherever you go, and I will bring you back to this land. I will not leave you until I have done what I have promised you. (Genesis 28:13-15)

Jacob left the land of promise twice, once fleeing from his angry brother, to return years later with two wives and twelve sons, and the second time fleeing with all his family to Egypt to escape a famine. This time, Jacob did not return alive. He died in Egypt and his body was taken back to the Promised Land to be buried beside Abraham and his father Isaac. Jacob's sons and descendants remained in Egypt and eventually became slaves to the Pharaoh there. After 400 years, God sent a deliverer to lead the "Children of Israel" out of bondage and back to the land God had promised to give them.

But the children of promise had a difficult time letting God do things his way. First they demanded a new god, one made of gold, rather than wait for the true God to tell them what he wanted them to do. After destroying their golden idol, Moses gave the Israelites the laws God had provided for them. It wasn't just the Ten Commandments, either. Almost half of the book of Exodus and nearly the entire books of Leviticus and Deuteronomy contain specific regulations for living and worship the Israelites were to follow. Being led by God to the land he had promised them, the Israelites grumbled against God and repeatedly wished they had stayed in Egypt. Then, at the very border of the Promised Land, the people refused to trust God and go in and take the land. God left the people to wander in the desert for forty years until all those who had rebelled against him died. Then he led their children into the land.

> See, I set before you today life and prosperity, death and destruction. For I command you today to love the Lord your God, to walk in his ways, and to keep his commands, decrees and laws; then you will live and increase, and the Lord your God will bless you in the land you are entering to possess. (Deuteronomy 30:15-16)

These were among the final words of Moses to the Children of Israel as they prepared their hearts and minds to do as God had commanded them and to enter the land God was giving them. Some 3000 years later these words would be echoed by the leader of another people who were being challenged to obey God's commands:

> Beloved there is now set before us life and good, death and evil, in that we are Commanded this day to love the Lord our God, and to love one another, to walk in his ways and to keep his Commandments and his Ordinance and his laws and the Articles of our Covenant with him that we may live and be multiplied, and that the Lord our God may bless us in the land whither we go to possess it: But if our hearts shall turn away so that we will not obey, but shall be seduced and worship other Gods, our pleasures, and profits, and serve them, it is propounded unto us this day, we shall surely perish out of the good Land whether we pass over this vast Sea to possess it.[1]

These were the words of John Winthrop, leader of the Puritan colonists of Massachusetts Bay Colony and their first governor in the New World. Like Moses, Winthrop reminded his people to obey God's laws and seek him first if the people would gain what God had promised them. But there was a material difference between the children of Israel and the Puritans of Massachusetts Bay that John Winthrop apparently did not realize. They had been given a different promise.

The Old Covenant

The covenant made with Israel at the threshold of the Promised Land was for Israel alone. God made it clear through the Old Testament prophets that Israel had been chosen out of all the nations for a special purpose, and so the promise to Israel was available to no other nation.

> For you are a people holy to the Lord your God. The Lord your God has chosen you out of all the peoples on the face of the earth to be his people, his treasured possession. (Deuteronomy 7:6)

> He has revealed his word to Jacob, his laws and decrees to Israel. He has done this for no other nation; they do not know his laws. Praise the Lord. (Psalm 147:19-20)

> You only have I chosen of all the families of the earth; therefore I will punish you for all your sins. (Amos 3:2)

Israel was given a promise of peace and prosperity if the nation obeyed God's laws and a promise of punishment and rejection if the nation turned from those laws. Although God judges all the nations for their sins, only Israel was given a promise of blessing for obedience. Why is this? It is because Israel was given a special *responsibility* by God. As one biblical scholar has put it, Israel had a special mission:

(1) to be the recipient and custodian of the true revelation of God (Exodus 3: Ps. 147:19-20; Rom. 3:1-2); (2) to exhibit to the world true religion and morality through her separation from other nations and by her obedience, righteousness, and holiness (Deut. 7:6; Lev. 20:4-26); and (3) to prepare the way for the Messiah (Gen. 12:1-3; 2 Sam. 7; Rom. 1:3; Gal. 3:16).[2]

The New Testament tells us that all the things that happened to the nation of Israel in the Old Testament, both the blessings and the punishments, "happened to them as examples and were written down as warnings for us, on whom the fulfillment of the ages has come" (1 Corinthians 10:11). All of the law, all of the prophecies, all of God's dealings with the Children of Israel pointed toward something that was coming: A New Covenant made possible only through the death and resurrection of Jesus Christ.

Does this mean God no longer blesses faithfulness? Are his promises of peace and prosperity not available to any other nation which exhibits "obedience, righteousness and holiness"? What about the belief of our founding fathers and many of our nation's leaders that God has called the United States for a special mission, too? The only possible means of answering these questions is to look at the New Covenant God made through his son, Jesus.

The New Covenant

The New Testament book of Hebrews very carefully lays out the purpose of the Old Covenant and how it is replaced by the new. On Mount Sinai, Moses was given the commandments by which the children of Israel were to live. The commandments contained not only laws of conduct, but also laws of sacrifice—including daily sacrifices of goats and calves whose blood was shed to cover the sins of the people. Although God had offered a blessing to the people if they obeyed the law, he knew beforehand they could not obey the law perfectly, so some payment for their disobedience would be necessary. But the blood of the sacrifices did not really take away the people's sins. It was written in Psalm 40:6, "Sacrifice and offering you did not desire…; burnt offerings and sin offerings you did not require." The law could not make the people righteous in God's eyes; neither could the animal sacrifices. Something more was required.

To paraphrase the writer of Hebrews:

> Day after day the priests stood and performed their religious duties, again and again offering the same sacrifices, which could never take away sins. But when Jesus had offered himself—for all time, one sacrifice for sins— he sat down at the right hand of God. By his one sacrifice he made perfect forever those who are being made holy. (Hebrews 10:11-14, paraphrased)

The children of Israel were blessed by God, not because of their perfect obedience to the law or because of the blood of sacrificial animals, but because of their faith in the perfect sacrifice God had promised was to come. That perfect sacrifice was Jesus, the Son of God who never sinned and was not deserving of any punishment. Because of Jesus' death and resurrection, our sins may be forgiven, not because we obey any law, but because we trust in him by faith. This is the essence of the New Covenant—faith in Jesus cleanses us perfectly from our sins and permits us to enter into the presence of God.

There are several material differences between the Old Covenant and the new. First, the New Covenant is available to "everyone who believes: first for the Jew, then for the Gentile" (Romans 1:16). This is the meaning of the promise made to Abraham that all the nations of the earth would be blessed through him (or, rather, his descendant, Jesus Christ). Second, where the Old Covenant was conditioned on obedience to God's laws, the New Covenant is conditioned on faith in God's grace. Third, where the Old Covenant promised peace and prosperity in the Promised Land, the New Covenant promises peace with God and entry into the Kingdom of God.

> The former regulation is set aside because it was weak and useless (for the law made nothing perfect), and a better hope is introduced, by which we draw near to God. (Hebrews 7:18)

> But now a righteousness from God, apart from law, has been made known, to which the Law and the Prophets testify. This righteousness from God comes through faith in Jesus Christ to all who believe. (Romans 3:21-22a)

"To all who believe." Not to any nation. Not to any particular group of people. But to all who believe. It is Christians who have been given a promise and a calling, not the United States of America. As Christians, we are justified by faith, not by obedience to any law. No matter how much the Puritans, or the founding fathers, or Americans today try to follow John Winthrop's advice and "love the Lord our God…and to keep his Commandments and his Ordinance and his laws," God has never promised to "bless us in the land whither we go to possess it." He has given us a different promise—and a better one. He has promised us the assurance of the forgiveness of our sins by his grace and an eternal home with him.

There is one more material difference between the Old Covenant and the new—our mission. Whereas Israel was "to exhibit to the world true religion and morality through her *separation* from other nations,"[3] Christians are to exhibit true religion and morality *within* the nations.

> Therefore go and make disciples of all nations, baptizing them in the name of the Father and of the Son and of the Holy Spirit, and teaching them to obey everything I have commanded you. And surely I am with you always, to the very end of the age. (Matthew 28:19-20)

These were the last words of Jesus Christ after his resurrection from the dead and before he left this world to join his father in Heaven. This is known as the Great Commission. We are commanded to spread the gospel of Christ and make new disciples within the nations. We are not told to make Christian nations! A nation cannot be made a disciple any more than it can be baptized. We are to reach people within the nations, including our own, and *after* they have become disciples of Jesus we are to teach them to follow his commandments. This is not a mission for the United States or for our president or Congress or the courts. It is a commandment given to you and to me, to our churches and fellow Christians. We cannot delegate God's command and hope to appease him by simply being a "religious" and law-abiding people. In fact, if we ever were to win all the people in the United States to Christianity, we would all have to leave! Our job here would be done, and we would need to go into other nations and make disciples and baptize and teach them.

Return Not to Egypt

Like the children of Israel, many Christians stand at the threshold of what God has promised and wish for something different. The children of Israel wanted to go back to Egypt. Although they were in slavery there, at least they were safe. Out in the wilderness, the Israelites had to trust God every day to provide their food and water and to lead them forward. God laid a great burden on their shoulders in the form of the Law, and commanded them to conquer a number of great nations and drive them out of the Promised Land. A life of slavery in Egypt suddenly seemed a lot easier.

> In the desert the whole community grumbled against Moses and Aaron. The
> Israelites said to them, "If only we had died by the Lord's hand in Egypt!
> There we sat around pots of meat and ate all the food we wanted, but you
> have brought us out into this desert to starve this entire assembly to death."
> (Exodus 16:2-3)

The apostle Paul tells us we were also slaves—slaves to the law. Like the children of Israel, we often find slavery to be more attractive than the freedom God offers.

> Before this faith came, we were held prisoners by the law, locked up until faith should be revealed. So the law was put in charge to lead us to Christ that we might be justified by faith. Now that faith has come, we are no longer under the supervision of the law.... But now that you know God—or rather are known by God —how is it that you are turning back to those weak and miserable principles? Do you wish to be enslaved by them all over again? (Galatians 3:23-25, 4:9)

Paul was writing to a group of Gentile believers who were being led in the wrong direction by some bad ideas. Jewish believers had come among them and told them that to please God they had to be circumcised and follow all the law just like the Jews. Believing in Jesus to take away their sins was not enough. Paul left no doubt in his letter to the Gentiles in Galatia that this was absolutely wrong! The whole point of the law had been to show the people they were sinners in need of salvation. The point of sacrifices and special observances was to show the people that a better sacrifice was needed. Jesus provided all that was necessary to free us, not only from the penalty for our sins, but also from the heavy requirements of laws and ceremonies.

> But now that you know God—or rather are known by God—how is it that you are turning back to those weak and miserable principles? Do you wish to be enslaved by them all over again? You are observing special days and months and seasons and years! I fear that somehow I have wasted my efforts on you.... It is for freedom that Christ has set us free. Stand firm, then, and do not let yourselves be burdened again by a yoke of slavery. (Galatians 4:9-11, 5:1)

The Jews had the law and their ceremonies of circumcision, sacrifices, and holy days. In America we also have our laws and our days of thanksgiving and prayer, our national motto (in God we Trust), our legislative chaplains, and our Pledge of Allegiance. These things cannot save us. They do not justify us before God. They don't even please God if we are doing them *for the wrong reason*. He has set us free from these things so we might worship him in truth, not just in some ceremonial show of outward obedience. Why then would we want to impose these empty ceremonies and useless laws of morality on the many in our country who do not know God? Wouldn't we do better to introduce them to his salvation?

But . . . .

If you are still not convinced, I can hardly blame you. We have all been raised to believe the United States was founded by God for a special purpose and God has given us a special blessing. Being "one nation, under God" has only been in the Pledge of Allegiance since 1954, but it has been a national theme since our founding. Have we been wrong all this time? Just briefly, let us consider some of these assumptions we have long held.

God brought the United States into being. Yes, he did. Doesn't that make us special? No, it doesn't. God brought *all* of the nations of the earth into being since the beginning of time.

> There is no authority except that which God has established. The authorities
> that exist have been established by God. (Romans 13:1)

> By me kings reign and rulers make laws that are just; by me princes govern,
> and all nobles who rule on earth. (Proverbs 8:15-16)

The United States was founded by God-fearing people who wanted to build a Christian community. Yes. And no. The Puritans who founded Plymouth Plantation and Massachusetts Bay Colony certainly came to the United States to build communities based on their religious beliefs, but they didn't come alone. Many others came to the shores of

America seeking wealth, land, and an opportunity to raise themselves socially in a way which was impossible in the impenetrable class structure of England and Europe. The difficult voyage to America and the rigors of living in an uncivilized land had little appeal to the gentry and nobility of England, but it had a great deal of appeal to the ambitious, the penniless, and the petty criminal who was given a choice of a hangman's noose or passage to the New World. Considering the brutal treatment of the native peoples, the explosive growth of the slave industry, and the constant battles over land between the English colonists and their French and Spanish neighbors, our first forefathers hardly exemplified a moral and peace-loving Christian people.

God blessed us by helping us win our independence. A number of our founding fathers considered it a miracle that the thrown-together, disorganized, and minimally armed colonial militia was able to defeat the greatest army of its time and win freedom from Britain. God's obvious favor of the colonists in battle proved to them that he agreed with their cause. They equated military success with divine approval, just as we continue to equate material blessings with God's favor. But there are several flaws in this assumption.

First, as explained above, God's promise of military success and material blessings was made to Israel and to no other nation. We cannot assume from that promise that God gives material blessings to other nations as a sign of his pleasure. God is sovereign, so everything that happens in this world happens as he chooses, including the triumphs of evil men and nations. Consider Nebuchadnezzar, the great king of Babylon. Although a pagan and an exceedingly proud man, God granted him authority over the greatest kingdom of his time—perhaps of all time. The prophet Daniel told Nebuchadnezzar, "The God of heaven has given you dominion and power and might and glory; in your hands he has placed mankind and the beasts of the field and the birds of the air. Wherever they live, he has made you ruler over them all" (Daniel 2:37-38). God used Nebuchadnezzar like "a sword, sharpened and polished" to bring about the fall of Jerusalem (Ezekiel 21:9). Then

God punished the great king for his pride (Daniel 4), and the mighty kingdom of Babylon was conquered by Cyrus of Persia, another pagan especially blessed and used by God (Isaiah 45).

Second, God tells us in his Word that material blessings are not always a measurement of righteousness. Consider Job, who was righteous in God's sight but was plagued with the loss of his property, the death of his children, and physical sufferings. When Job's friends assumed his misfortunes were a punishment from God, God was angry with them for not saying what was right about him (Job 42:7). Consider also Jesus' parable of the landowner who hired workers throughout the day to work in his vineyard. At the end of the day the landowner gave the same amount of pay to the men who had worked all day as he gave to those who worked only one hour. In responding to the complaints of the men who worked longer, the landowner replied:

> Friend, I am not being unfair to you. Didn't you agree to work for a certain amount? Take your pay and go. I want to give the man who was hired last the same as I gave you. Don't I have the right to do what I want with my own money? Or are you envious because I am generous? (Matthew 20:13-15)

Jesus used this parable to illustrate the point that God is not keeping score and doling out to each person and each nation the reward or punishment they have earned. If this were true, we would be in big trouble, because "all have sinned and come short of the glory of God" (Romans 3:23), and we are all deserving of nothing but eternal punishment. But God "causes his sun to rise on the evil and the good, and sends rain on the righteous and the unrighteous" (Matthew 5:45).

Our nation was founded on Christian principles. Life, liberty, and the pursuit of happiness. A republican form of government. Freedom and equality. These are supposed to be gifts from God that were given to the United States to share with the world. This is what truly sets us apart from the other nations of the world. Isn't it?

I'm afraid it would take another book to fully address this question, but for a few minutes just think about what God has to say about life, liberty, and equality in the Bible—not under the Old Covenant, but under the New. Where in the New Testament does God tell us to consider our lives to be a gift we should treasure? Did not Jesus say "whoever wants to save his life will lose it, but whoever loses his life for me will find it"? (Matthew 16:25). Did not Paul say "I have been crucified with Christ and I no longer live, but Christ lives in me"? (Galatians 2:20). And where are we told to value equality? Instead we are told: "Do nothing out of selfish ambition or vain conceit, but in humility consider others better than yourselves" (Philippians 2:3). Wives are told to be submissive to their husbands (Ephesians 5:22). Slaves are told to be pleasing to their masters (Titus 2:9). We are encouraged to be content in all circumstances, "whether well fed or hungry, whether living in plenty or in want" (Philippians 4:12).

The Bible describes our lives here on earth like grass that withers and flowers that fall (Isaiah 40:6-8) and like a "mist that appears for a little while and then vanishes" (James 4:14). It is not an earthly life God wants us to desire and cherish, but eternal life with him. It is not freedom from oppression God promises, but freedom from sin and the requirements of the law. It is not equality among men God offers, but equality among fellow Christians.

> You are all sons of God through faith in Christ Jesus, for all of you who were baptized into Christ have clothed yourselves with Christ. There is neither Jew nor Greek, slave nor free, male nor female, for you are all one in Christ Jesus. If you belong to Christ, then you are Abraham's seed, and heirs according to the promise. (Galatians 3:26-29)

The True Promise

"All people on earth will be blessed through you" (Genesis 12:3). This promise from God to Abraham is his promise to us as well, and to all who become children of the promise through faith in Jesus Christ. We who hold the keys of God's kingdom in our hands should be more concerned with the Great Commission than with the Ten Commandments. We should be actively shining the light of God's love in the world through service to others instead of demanding that others change their lives for our comfort. We should be inviting the lost to put their lives under God's control instead of reinforcing a false belief that we are a privileged nation "under God." We need to throw away the crutches of moral laws and religious ceremonies that do not justify us in God's sight and stand on faith alone. We need to show the world that true religion needs neither the support nor the approval of the governments of men in order to survive and thrive. We need to build a firm wall of separation between our flawed, human government and our divine calling of worship to God.

> Give to Caesar what is Caesar's, and to God what is God's. (Matthew 22:21)

> For here we do not have an enduring city, but we are looking for the city that is to come. (Hebrews 13:14)

Chapter 8

Pilgrims

With mutual embraces and many tears, they took their leaves one of
another, which proved to be the last leave to many of them…
But they knew they were pilgrims, and looked not much on those things,
but lifted up their eyes to the heavens, their dearest country,
and quieted their spirits.
~ William Bradford, 1617[1] ~

Before John Winthrop arrived in New England with his Massachusetts Puritans and his vision of a "city upon a hill," there was another group of dissident Christians who made the difficult journey across the Atlantic. Known as Separatists because they believed it was better to separate from the established Church of England than to follow its decrees, these Christians made a decision to leave England and find a place where they could worship God, not according to the dictates of a king or queen, but according to their own understanding of the Bible and God's will for them. Escaping from England to the Netherlands, the Separatists found more religious freedom, but many other difficulties. Eventually, part of the group decided to take the very bold step of sailing to the New World and starting a colony.

They were English subjects still. They came to America with a land patent from the king and with financial backing from English merchants. They did not deny the authority of the king or of Parliament over the civil aspects of their lives. But on the question of their duty to God, they could not accept the authority of their government over the authority of God's Word. Since the King of England did not agree with them on this point, they chose to physically separate themselves not only from the Church of England but from their native country as well. These men and women, known to history as the Pilgrims, risked everything and suffered much to find a place where they could plant their own church and live their lives according to the laws of God.

Live As Pilgrims

William Bradford called his brave group of Separatists "pilgrims" after those dauntless Christians who had, for centuries past, left their homes and traveled to distant lands to visit some holy shrine, or the site of a miraculous happening, or a place where the bones or belongings of saints could be found—a place where they could feel closer to God. The Pilgrims who set sail on the Mayflower also wanted to feel closer to God. They were able to leave behind their houses and land in England because they knew that country was only a temporary home. And they were able to endure the hardships and deprivations of the New World because they knew it, as well, was not their final destination. Instead, they "lifted up their eyes to the heavens, their dearest country, and quieted their spirits."[2]

As Christians, we should live in this world—*wherever* we live in this world—like the Pilgrims of Plymouth Plantation. We should recognize our place of residence here is temporary. Our nationality is temporary. Our true citizenship is not in any nation on the earth, but in the Kingdom of God, both now and for eternity. We should not hold too tightly or be too concerned for anything on this earth. For our treasure and our home is in heaven.

This is not to say we should have nothing to do with the world or with the laws and politics of the nation we reside in. God has placed each one of us on the earth for a time and for a reason, and he has placed us within the nations of the earth where we may live and work, even while we look heavenward to our eventual home. When Jacob and his sons and their families traveled to Egypt to escape the famine in their homeland, they settled in there. "They acquired property there and were fruitful and increased greatly in number" (Genesis 47:27). Their descendants would remain in Egypt for 400 years, but they never forgot that Egypt was not their home. Centuries later, when the Israelites were taken into captivity in Babylon, God told the people they would live in that land for 70 years before he would return them to the Promised Land. While in a foreign land, however, he expected them to go on living.

> Build houses and settle down; plant gardens and eat what they produce. Marry and have sons and daughters; find wives for your sons and give your daughter in marriage, so that they too may have sons and daughters. Increase in number there; do not decrease. (Jeremiah 29:5-6)

God went on then to make an extraordinary pronouncement:

> Also, seek the peace and prosperity of the city to which I have carried you into exile. Pray to the Lord for it, because if it prospers, you too will prosper. (Jeremiah 29:7)

Jesus also told his disciples he would prepare a place for them in his "Father's house" and would someday return for them after he had gone away (John 14:2-3). Yet he meant for them to take an active part in this world until he returned to take them to the next. Jesus instructed his followers to pay their taxes to Rome and to the leaders of the temple (Matthew 22:17-21; 17:24-27). He set an example of caring and service by feeding the hungry and healing the sick, and he taught us how we ought to live with each other in a sinful world (See Matthew 5-7). Then, in his last words, he sent his people into all the world to "go and make disciples," promising to go with them wherever they went "to the very end of the age" (Matthew 28:19-20).

Of course, our world has changed in many ways since Jesus walked on the earth and gave his Sermon on the Mount. How are we to live in this time and in this place? And how are we to relate to a government and a society so different from any that existed when the Bible was written?

Live by the Word of God

Even though the Bible was written long ago in a world which seems vastly different than the one we know today, we must remember it was written under the direction of the Spirit of God, the same Spirit who has existed for all time and who lives within all true Christians today. The Four Gospels, which tell the story of Jesus' life and teachings, and the letters of the apostles are filled with directions for living a godly life in an ungodly world. In addition to specific instructions, there are general principles and many examples given to us to learn from and to apply to our own lives. Among God's instructions, there are at least four which apply to how we should live as residents or citizens of a particular nation—even 2000 years after they were written.

Submit:

> Everyone must submit himself to the governing authorities, for there is no authority except that which God has established. The authorities that exist have been established by God. Consequently, he who rebels against the authority is rebelling against what God has instituted, and those who do so will bring judgment on themselves. (Romans 13:1-2)

Support and Respect:

> This is also why you pay taxes, for the authorities are God's servants, who give their full time to governing. Give everyone what you owe him: If you

owe taxes, pay taxes; if revenue, then revenue; if respect, then respect; if honor, then honor. (Romans 13:6-7)

Pray:

I urge, then, first of all, that requests, prayers, intercession and thanksgiving be made for everyone—for kings and all those in authority, that we may live peaceful and quiet lives in all godliness and holiness. (1 Timothy 2:1-2)

Note that none of these instructions require that you like the person or persons in authority over you, or even that you agree with them. The "governing authorities" Paul told the early churches to pray for and submit to include the government of Rome, which would eventually take Paul's life for preaching the gospel of Christ.

The one exception to submitting to a governing authority and obeying its laws is when those laws conflict directly with the commands of God. Two examples of this are given in the book of Daniel where Shadrach, Meshach, and Abednego intentionally disobeyed the king of Babylon's order to worship a golden image, and Daniel intentionally disobeyed the king's order to pray to no one but the king (Daniel 3 and 6). Although these men knew God could deliver them from punishment for breaking the king's law if he so chose, they were willing to submit to that punishment (death in a fiery furnace for Shadrach, Meshach, and Abednego and being thrown to hungry lions for Daniel) rather than serve false gods or give false worship.

Stewardship:

In addition to these specific instructions, we are reminded to be good stewards of everything that has been entrusted to us.

Whoever can be trusted with very little can also be trusted with much, and whoever is dishonest with very little will also be dishonest with much. So if you have not been trustworthy in handling worldly wealth, who will trust you with true riches? And if you have not been trustworthy with someone else's property, who will give you property of your own? (Luke 16:10-12)

Jesus, who often referred to himself as a servant, told several parables about servants and stewards, including one about a master who left on a journey after leaving three of his servants with different sums of money. Two of the servants put the money to work and made a profit, while the third servant hid the money away out of fear of losing it. When the master returned, he rewarded the two servants who had wisely used the money entrusted to them, and he took everything away from the servant who hid the money away (Matthew 25:14-30; Luke 19:12-26). Like the wise servants, we should make good use of the things God has entrusted to us for the sake of his glory.

What has God entrusted to us? Prosperity. Peace. The rights recognized by our government. Our political freedoms. We should not consider these things as rights granted by God or rewards earned by our good behavior. They are gifts of God lent to us for a time and for a purpose. If we are faithful with these things on earth then we can expect to be entrusted with much more in heaven.

How are we to use these gifts? Consider Paul, who more than once stood up to civil authorities who were trying to silence his message by reminding them of his rights as a Roman citizen (Acts 16:36-38, 22:25-29). Paul was not afraid of being beaten or thrown in jail. He had already suffered many beatings, jailings, and other hardships. But he did not hesitate to rely on his right to fair treatment from the government when he saw that it could further his work. Jesus also spoke out against the injustice of the accusations made against him (John 18:19-23), but he submitted peacefully to an unfair trial and to his own execution because he knew it was God's will.

In the United States of America we have the ability to vote, to run for office, to bring our grievances before the courts, and to speak out on issues and try to persuade others to join us in our beliefs. These are incredible gifts, and we must use them wisely. Not for our own comfort or personal gain, but in a way that is pleasing to our Master.

Live in the Spirit

Paul said, "It is for freedom that Christ has set us free. Stand firm, then, and do not let yourselves be burdened again by a yoke of slavery" (Galatians 5:1). But Paul went on to explain this freedom in the same letter:

> You, my brothers, were called to be free. But do not use your freedom to indulge the sinful nature; rather, serve one another in love…. Live by the Spirit, and you will not gratify the desires of the sinful nature… The acts of the sinful nature are obvious: sexual immorality, impurity and debauchery; idolatry and witchcraft; hatred, discord, jealousy, fits of rage, selfish ambition, dissensions, factions and envy; drunkenness, orgies, and the like…. But the fruit of the Spirit is love, joy, peace, patience, kindness, goodness, faithfulness, gentleness and self-control. Against such things there is no law. (Galatians 5:13, 16, 19-23)

Avoiding idolatry, drunkenness. and orgies is easy enough to understand, and we can all work on exhibiting patience, kindness, and self-control. But what about the "big questions" of life? Who should I vote for in the next election? Should I participate in political parties or other organizations trying to make a change in America? Should I allow my children to attend public schools where they are taught about evolution and humanism? Should I even say the Pledge of Allegiance to the American flag, or by doing so am I letting my country take the rightful place of my God?

These are all difficult questions. We are told in the Bible to obey the laws of our government as long as they do not directly conflict with the law of God. That raises some difficulties at times, but in a country such as the United States, where we have so much freedom to do as we choose, it is much more difficult to decide how to use our freedoms.

When I thought of this problem, I couldn't help but think of the story of a crippled man who was healed by Peter not long after the resurrection of Jesus.

> One day Peter and John were going up to the temple at the time of prayer—at three in the afternoon. Now a man crippled from birth was being carried to the temple gate called Beautiful, where he was put every day to beg from those going into the temple courts. When he saw Peter and John about to enter, he asked them for money. Peter looked straight at him, as did John. Then Peter said, "Look at us!" So the man gave them his attention, expecting to get something from them.
>
> Then Peter said, "Silver or gold I do not have, but what I have I give you. In the name of Jesus Christ of Nazareth, walk." Taking him by the right hand, he helped him up, and instantly the man's feet and ankles became strong. He jumped to his feet and began to walk. Then he went with them into the temple courts, walking and jumping, and praising God. (Acts 3:1-8)

"He went with them…walking and jumping and praising God." His story ends there, but his life had just begun. Have you ever wondered what that formerly crippled man did then? Did he know the way to walk home, since he had never walked there by himself before? He had probably never sat in a chair for a meal, or helped around the house, or possibly even put on shoes before. It is doubtful he had ever done any kind of job. Now that he couldn't beg at the temple anymore, what was he supposed to do?

We might all imagine at times what it would be like to have our health or our property or our freedoms taken away from us, but few of us ever consider how we would live if we suddenly had more freedom and abilities than we ever had before. With new freedoms and abilities comes new responsibilities, and we might not know how to handle that. If we are short-sighted like the Israelites, we might want to go back to a simpler way of life where we know exactly what is expected of us and how much (or how little) we have to do to get through the day. Or we can be like the crippled man given the use of his legs for the first time in his life and just leap up and go!

When the Israelites were led out of their social/political slavery in Egypt, God gave them the law and ceremonies like crutches to hold them up and help them walk. When God leads you out of the spiritual slavery of sin, he gives you something more.

> And I will ask the Father, and he will give you another Counselor to be with you forever—the Spirit of truth. The world cannot accept him, because it neither sees him nor knows him. But you know him, for he lives with you and will be in you. (John 14:16-17)

The crutches of strict obedience to the law and to ceremonial ritual are no longer needed. It is time to throw them down and walk in the Spirit by faith. Not all the questions of life have direct answers in the Bible, but God has given us his Spirit to help us apply the principles found there and to learn from the examples. When we are confronted with difficult questions about how to use our freedoms we should pray for wisdom, seek counsel from those gifted by God to teach his Word, and carefully search his Word and our own hearts to make sure we are focused on doing things his way, not ours.

> If any of you lacks wisdom, he should ask God, who gives generously to all without finding fault, and it will be given to him. (James 1:5)

Do your best to present yourself to God as one approved, a workman who does not need to be ashamed and who correctly handles the word of truth. (2 Timothy 2:15)

Live Under Two Governments

Finally, we must remember that we are members of two different societies, or cultures, here on earth: our civil society and our brothers and sisters in Christ who make up the Church. God's instructions for how we should live in relation to these two societies are different. Paul wrote to the church in Corinth:

I have written you in my letter not to associate with sexually immoral people—not at all meaning the people of this world who are immoral, or the greedy and swindlers, or idolaters. In that case you would have to leave this world. But now I am writing you that you must not associate with anyone who calls himself a brother but is sexually immoral or greedy, an idolater or a slanderer, a drunkard or a swindler. With such a man do not even eat. What business is it of mine to judge those outside the church? Are you not to judge those inside? God will judge those outside. Expel the wicked man from among you. (1 Corinthians 5:9-13)

God will judge those outside the church. It is not our business to try and change our nation or the people in it or to sit in judgment over them. It is our business to spread the gospel of Christ. Anything that deters from the gospel, including our own ungodly conduct which throws our message into disrepute, should be avoided. Anything which helps the gospel should be pursued. Within the church, on the other hand, we are to seek purity and morality, living to a much higher standard than the world aspires to so we might truly be a light in the darkness.

It is good for people who are Christians to work in government service, to become lawyers, or to be involved in the political process. It is good for all Christians to be informed voters and active members of their societies. We should all do what we can to maintain the freedoms and rights we have in this nation—while we have them—because God has entrusted those things to us for the purpose of spreading the gospel of Christ. We should support our government and vote in such a way as to preserve peace within the nation and to promote justice, as these are probably the two most important functions of civil governments. (See Deuteronomy 16:18-20; Proverbs 29:4; Jeremiah 29:7; Romans 13:3-5; and I Timothy 2:1-2). But we must remember our civil government is a government of fallen human beings, no more or less able than any other government of human beings to serve God or to glorify him. That is the role of the Church, not the State, and we are better off keeping the two separate.

Conclusion

As I have written this final chapter, the last few weeks of the 2004 presidential election have passed. George W. Bush has been reelected as President of the United States, and a Republican Congress has been guaranteed. A number of Justices on the Supreme Court are likely to retire in the coming years and be replaced by new men and women of either a conservative or a liberal bent. Many important issues are set to be decided—or reconsidered—in the next four years, such as abortion rights, gay marriage, America's role in the world, and the use of God's name in the Pledge of Allegiance. Conservative voters are celebrating, hoping for movement towards a more moral society, and liberals are vowing to fight back in the next election, determined to secure the right to do as they choose instead of bowing to a fundamentalist majority. But as Senator John Kerry so eloquently stated in his concession speech after the election, "In an American election there are no losers, because whether or not our candidates are successful, the next morning we all wake up as Americans."

He is right. We are all Americans. As Christians we have as much a share in our government and our nation as any other person. But we also have a share in something much greater. I love my country. I am absolutely in awe of the work done by our founding fathers in creating a government so well balanced and limited, and yet capable of growing and adapting right along with the growth and change of the nation. I hold in deep respect the men and women who have fought and died for our liberty, for our freedoms, and for our safety and for the many who serve today to keep those gifts secure. And yet, in the balance, I must consider all of these things as empty and meaningless when compared to the riches of the blessing of God's love for me and his plan for my life.

If I have left you at the end of this book with more questions about your role as a Christian-American than you had when you started it, then I have accomplished the work I set out to do. There are no simple answers. There is no blueprint for a perfect nation or a manifesto for Christian politics. But there is a living and active God who has given us his Word and his Spirit to help us make the decisions we need to make each day. And there is also a promise that God will work things out for our good as well as his if we just trust him.

> Therefore I tell you, do not worry about your life, what you will eat or drink; or about your body, what you will wear. Is not life more important than food, and the body more important than clothes? Look at the birds of the air; they do not sow or reap or store away in barns, and yet your heavenly Father feeds them…. And why do you worry about clothes? See how the lilies of the field grow. They do not labor or spin. Yet I tell you that not even Solomon in all his splendor was dressed like one of these…. So do not worry, saying, "What shall we eat?" or "What shall we wear?" For the pagans run after all these things, and your heavenly Father knows that you need them. But seek first his kingdom and his righteousness, and all these things will be given to you as well. (Matthew 6:25-33)

Seek God. Stay focused on his will. Stop judging others outside the Church. Spread the gospel. Don't worry too much about the affairs of our nation, which is only your temporary home. Trust God. And "all these things will be given to you as well."

Chapter 9
And Now

I do not believe that the phrase "under God" in the Pledge converts its recital into a "religious exercise".... Instead, it is a declaration of belief in allegiance and loyalty to the United States flag and the Republic that it represents....; participants promise fidelity to our flag and our Nation, not to any particular God, faith, or church.
~ Chief Justice William Rehnquist, 2004[1] ~

Much has changed in our nation and on the Supreme Court since the Pledge of Allegiance case was decided in 2004. In fact, only three of the Justices who participated in that case were still on the Court by the end of 2019. Other cases have been decided since then involving the Establishment Clause and the Free Exercise Clause. As promised in this book's introduction, I would now like to jump back in and bring you up to date on court cases decided between 2005, when the first version of this book came out, and 2019.

"Under God" and "In God We Trust"

Michael Newdow has not been silent since the Supreme Court ruled against him in 2004 and overturned the Ninth Circuit's decision finding the Pledge of Allegiance unconstitutional. Newdow went right home and found two other plaintiffs (the anonymous Jan Doe and Jan Roe) to join him in suing the Rio Linda School District in California for requiring the recitation of the Pledge of Allegiance in front of their children contrary to the parents' atheistic beliefs. Newdow also sued the United States of America, Congress, the Secretary of the Treasury, the Director of the United States Mint, and the Director of the Bureau of Engraving and Printing requesting an injunction against printing coins with the motto "In God We Trust."

In the Pledge of Allegiance case, the lower court found at least one of the plaintiffs had standing to bring the case. The court ruled in favor of the plaintiffs, using the Ninth Circuit's decision in the original Newdow case as precedent (even though it was overturned by the United States Supreme Court).[2] The Ninth Circuit reversed. Starting fresh, and reviewing the Establishment Clause issue under three different tests, the court found that a required "teacher-led recitation of the Pledge of Allegiance…is constitutional."[3]

> We hold that the Pledge of Allegiance does not violate the Establishment Clause because Congress' ostensible and predominant purpose was to inspire patriotism and that the context of the Pledge—its wording as a whole, the preamble to the statute, and this nation's history—demonstrate that it is a predominantly patriotic exercise. For these reasons, the phrase "one Nation under God" does not turn this patriotic exercise into a religious activity. [4]

In Newdow's other case, the Ninth Circuit upheld a district court ruling dismissing the case. Quoting an earlier case as precedent, the court stated:

> It is quite obvious that the national motto and the slogan on coinage and currency 'In God We Trust' has nothing whatsoever to do with the establishment of religion. Its use is of a patriotic or ceremonial character and bears no true resemblance to a governmental sponsorship of a religious

exercise…. While 'ceremonial' and 'patriotic' may not be particularly apt words to describe the category of the national motto, it is excluded from First Amendment significance because the motto has no theological or ritualistic impact. As stated by the Congressional report, it has 'spiritual and psychological value' and 'inspirational quality.'[5]

Undaunted, Newdow tried a new line of attack against public expressions of religion. In 2001 and 2005, Newdow sued over the prayers said at President George W. Bush's inaugurations. He brought suit again in 2009 to prevent any reference to God at President Barack Obama's first inauguration. He lost each time.[6]

Monuments, Prayers, and other Establishment Clause Cases

While none of Newdow's new cases reached the Supreme Court, the Court has not been silent on the First Amendment Religion Clauses. In 2005, one year after the Pledge case, the Supreme Court ruled on two similar cases, reaching different decisions. In one case, a six-foot-high monument displaying the Ten Commandments stood in a park around the Texas state capitol building along with 16 other monuments and 21 historical markers. In the other case, the Ten Commandments were displayed in two Kentucky county courthouses, surrounded by other documents with religious references. Deciding the two cases on the same day, the Supreme Court ruled that the "passive" placement of the monument in Texas did not offend the constitutional prohibition against the establishment of religion[7] but the Ten Commandments display in Kentucky violated the Constitution because it was done with a religious purpose.[8] The Court relied on "the principle that the 'First Amendment mandates governmental neutrality between religion and religion, and between religion and nonreligion.'"[9] According to the Court, a six-foot monument set among many other kinds of monuments in a park outside governmental buildings appeared neutral on religion, while a large piece of paper on a wall inside a courthouse did not.

Also in 2005, the Supreme Court upheld the constitutionality of a federal law which prevents government officials from imposing "a substantial burden on the religious exercise" of federal prisoners unless the burden furthers "a compelling governmental interest," and does so by "the least restrictive means."[10] Previously, the Court had ruled that prison officials may infringe on the constitutional rights of inmates whenever the infringing regulation "is valid [and] reasonably related to legitimate penological interests"—a very low standard for the government to live up to.[11] Under the new law upheld by the Court, federal prisons must now show a compelling reason to infringe on prisoners' religious rights and prevent them from practicing their chosen religions.

Since 2005, the Court has remanded some Establishment Clause cases on procedural grounds while refusing to discuss the constitutional issues[12] and has refused to review other cases over the objection of some members of the Court.[13] In one case involving the use of white crosses to mark locations where state highway patrol officers had been killed, Justice Thomas lamented the Court's refusal to provide clear guidance on how Establishment Clause cases should be decided:

> Today the Court rejects an opportunity to provide clarity to an Establishment Clause jurisprudence in shambles. A sharply divided Court of Appeals for the Tenth Circuit has declared unconstitutional a private association's efforts to memorialize slain police officers with white roadside crosses, holding that the crosses convey to a reasonable observer that the State of Utah is endorsing Christianity. The Tenth Circuit's opinion is one of the latest in a long line of "religious display" decisions that, because of this Court's nebulous Establishment Clause analyses, turn on little more than "judicial predilections." … Because our jurisprudence has confounded the lower courts and rendered the constitutionality of displays of religious imagery on government property anyone's guess, I would grant certiorari.[14]

In 2014, the Court did decide a case on its merits, but not one dealing with religious displays. In *Town of Greece v. Galloway*, the Court took another look at the issue of government-sponsored prayer, this time regarding local clergy praying at the beginning of town board meetings. Reaffirming the idea that "the Establishment Clause must be interpreted 'by reference to historical practices and understandings,'" the Court upheld the practice of inviting local clergy from different religious denominations to open the board meetings in prayer without requiring the prayers to be generic and nonsectarian.[15]

> Legislative prayer, while religious in nature, has long been understood as compatible with the Establishment Clause. As practiced by Congress since the framing of the Constitution, legislative prayer lends gravity to public business, reminds lawmakers to transcend petty differences in pursuit of a higher purpose, and expresses a common aspiration to a just and peaceful society…. The First Amendment is not a majority rule, and government may not seek to define permissible categories of religious speech. Once it invites prayer into the public sphere, government must permit a prayer giver to address his or her own God or gods as conscience dictates, unfettered by what an administrator or judge considers to be nonsectarian…. So long as the town maintains a policy of nondiscrimination, the Constitution does not require it to search beyond its borders for non-Christian prayer givers in an effort to achieve religious balancing.[16]

Of course, it probably helped that the town allowed a Jewish layman, the chairman of the local Baha'i temple, and a Wiccan priestess to pray, in addition to the Christian ministers who represented the majority of the town's population.

Perhaps the most interesting aspect of that decision was the Court's deference to the long-standing historical practice of opening public hearings with prayer. Relying on *Marsh*, an earlier legislative prayer case, the Court stressed the non-religious aspect of the admittedly religious act of praying:

> *Marsh* must not be understood as permitting a practice that would amount to a constitutional violation if not for its historical foundation. The case teaches instead that the Establishment Clause must be interpreted "by reference to historical practices and understandings" and that the decision of the First Congress to "provid[e] for the appointment of chaplains only days after approving language for the First Amendment demonstrates that the Framers considered legislative prayer a benign acknowledgment of religion's role in society."[17]

This idea of deferring to historical practices was reiterated by the Court in 2019 when it upheld the constitutionality of a large cross maintained by the state of Maryland as part of a World War I memorial.[18] Finding four reasons why earlier tests were unhelpful in determining the constitutionality of long-established "monuments, symbols, and practices," the Court concluded that "the passage of time gives rise to a strong presumption of constitutionality."[19] In support of this idea, the Court listed other symbols and practices originally associated with Christianity which have lost much of their religious meaning over time, such as cities named after saints and angels (San Diego, San Francisco, Santa Barbara, Los Angeles, etc.), the crosses which appear in Maryland's flag, and the motto in Arizona's seal (*Ditat Deus*—God Enriches).

These two cases will undoubtedly be referred to if the Pledge of Allegiance and the National Motto are challenged again in the future. The question will be how long must a practice or symbol be in use before it can be presumed constitutional?

Religious Freedom and the Hobby Lobby Decision

In 2014, the Supreme Court addressed the issue of religious freedom in *Burwell v. Hobby Lobby Stores*.[20] It is important to note, though, that the *Hobby Lobby* case is not a First Amendment case. Although the plaintiffs raised First Amendment claims, the case was decided on the basis of a federal statute and not the Constitution.

In 1990, the Supreme Court issued a decision in *Employment Division v. Smith*, removing almost all protection for individuals under the First Amendment Free Exercise Clause.[21] Any law of general applicability could be used to stop a person from acting according to their religious convictions or to force a person to act in a way opposed to their religious beliefs. In 1993, Congress passed the Religious Freedom Restoration Act (RFRA) to counteract that ruling and require that any governmental action imposing a substantial burden on religious exercise must serve a compelling government interest.[22] In 1997, the Court ruled that RFRA could be used to limit the conduct of the federal government but not the states.[23] In 2000, Congress passed another, similar law, this time giving a broad definition of "exercise of religion" instead of referring to "the exercise of religion under the First Amendment."[24]

In the *Hobby Lobby* case, the owners of three businesses objected on religious grounds to the new Patient Protection and Affordable Care Act of 2010, specifically its requirement that companies pay for insurance coverage for contraceptives for their employees. The Court employed the federal statutes mentioned above to determine if a compelling governmental reason existed for requiring these companies to pay for the objectionable insurance. The real issue in the case was whether a *company*—as opposed to a person— had any right to exercise religious freedoms. By a vote of 5 to 4, the Court found that these plaintiffs, "three closely held for-profit corporations," did have religious freedoms protected by the federal statutes. Since the government had no compelling reason not to exempt these companies (as the 2010 act already exempted churches and religious nonprofit organizations), the companies could not be compelled to pay for certain contraception coverage over their religious objections.[25]

In 2016, the Court heard another appeal about the Patient Protection and Affordable Care Act. Under the act, exempt organizations are still required to provide insurance coverage for contraceptives, including ones that cause abortions, but the government pays for that portion of the insurance rather than the employer. In *Zubick v. Burwell,* the Court heard from several organizations who didn't want to provide such coverage, no matter who was paying for it. The Court remanded the case with the understanding that the government agencies involved would create a new procedure for providing contraceptive coverage directly to the employees of exempt organizations without the organizations being involved.[26] The following year, the Department of Health and Human Services created a new rule to exempt such organizations from including contraceptives in their insurance plans at all. However, that rule was overturned by the Ninth Circuit in October 2019, leaving the entire issue in doubt again.[27]

Religious Freedom and the Same-Sex Marriage Case

Another case that ignited controversy throughout the nation and renewed discussions about freedom of religion was *Obergefell v. Hodges.*[28] In June 2015, the Supreme Court overturned the laws of Michigan, Kentucky, Ohio, and Tennessee defining marriage as a union between one man and one woman and found that the fundamental right to marry, protected by the Fourteenth Amendment, extends to the choice to marry a person of the same sex. Four Justices dissented from the decision, pointing out that neither the ruling nor the reasoning followed any previous interpretation of the Constitution.

> Petitioners make strong arguments rooted in social policy and considerations of fairness. They contend that same-sex couples should be allowed to affirm their love and commitment through marriage, just like

opposite-sex couples…. Although the policy arguments for extending marriage to same-sex couples may be compelling, the legal arguments for requiring such an extension are not. The fundamental right to marry does not include a right to make a State change its definition of marriage. And a State's decision to maintain the meaning of marriage that has persisted in every culture throughout human history can hardly be called irrational.[29]

Irrational or not, the right of states to define marriage as between one man and one woman was overruled, making same-sex marriages legal in every state.

While ruling in favor of the petitioners in the case, the Court recognized the valid position of those with religious objections to same-sex marriage:

Finally, it must be emphasized that religions, and those who adhere to religious doctrines, may continue to advocate with utmost, sincere conviction that, by divine precepts, same-sex marriage should not be condoned. The First Amendment ensures that religious organizations and persons are given proper protection as they seek to teach the principles that are so fulfilling and so central to their lives and faiths, and to their own deep aspirations to continue the family structure they have long revered. The same is true of those who oppose same-sex marriage for other reasons. In turn, those who believe allowing same-sex marriage is proper or indeed essential, whether as a matter of religious conviction or secular belief, may engage those who disagree with their view in an open and searching debate.[30]

That debate quickly centered on what the Court did *not* say. If it is constitutionally protected to believe and teach that same-sex marriage is wrong, is it also constitutionally protected to *act* in accordance with those beliefs? This question was put to the test in different places. In Kentucky, a county clerk named Kim Davis refused to issue marriage licenses to same-sex couples, claiming she was morally opposed to having her name on the license as required by state law. Davis was charged with contempt of court for refusing to comply with her governmental duties and served five days in jail. The owner of a bakery in Colorado was sued for refusing to make a cake for a same-sex wedding, and a florist in Washington was sued for refusing to provide flowers for a same-sex wedding. Both the baker and the florist lost their cases due to state laws which make it illegal to discriminate on the basis of sexual orientation.

In 2018, the Supreme Court considered the cases of the Colorado baker and the Washington florist. In the case of the baker, the Court reversed the decision of the Colorado courts because the Colorado Civil Rights Commission failed to exercise religious neutrality in its decision against the baker. The Court found that the Commission showed open hostility to the baker and his religious beliefs and its ruling was inconsistent with other cases where it found it was not illegal discrimination to refuse to make a cake *opposed* to same-sex unions.[31] Two months later, the Court remanded the florist's case, instructing the Washington Supreme Court to reconsider the case in light of it's ruling in favor of the baker.[32]

While reversing one case and remanding the other, the Court did not make any findings on the constitutionality of refusing service to same-sex couples based on the free exercise of religion or freedom of speech. In fact, the Court reaffirmed its earlier decisions which held that "such objections do not allow business owners and other actors in the economy and in society to deny protected persons equal access to goods and services under a neutral and generally applicable public accommodations law."[33] In other words, these cases should not be seen as a change in the Court's position that the Free Exercise Clause does not allow a person to opt-out of laws they don't agree with because of their religious beliefs.

On June 6, 2019, the Washington Supreme Court ruled that no hostility against religion was shown in the florist's case. The decision will likely be appealed again to the Supreme Court, forcing the Court to finally consider the constitutional claims on their merits.[34]

Political and Cultural Shifts

As these cases show, there appears to be a shift in the way the Supreme Court is viewing the Free Exercise and Establishment Clauses, with greater deference being shown to religious beliefs and traditions. Since 2004, when the Pledge of Allegiance case was decided, four Justices have been added to the Court by Republican presidents, resulting in a 5-4 majority of conservative-leaning Justices on the bench at the end of 2019. Several states have reacted to the shift by passing new anti-abortion laws they hope may lead to an eventual overturning of *Roe v. Wade*, a case that interests Christians as much as any religious freedom case.[35]

President Donald Trump made religious liberty a talking point for his 2016 campaign and a priority for his administration, as evidenced by the 2017 Religious Liberty Executive Order and the 2018 White House Faith and Opportunity Initiative.[36] Of course, a U.S. President can serve for no more than eight years, and the next person in the office may have very different priorities. But the conservative majority on the Supreme Court created by President Trump's recent appointments could last a long time. Supreme Court Justices serve until they resign or die.

Evangelical Christians overwhelmingly voted for Trump in 2016, based at least in part on his support of conservative values. But over time, support for those values among the American people has been dwindling.

- In 2005, 79% of the US adult population considered themselves to be Christian. That's a considerable majority, but a drop from 93% in 1954 when the words "under God" were added to the Pledge of Allegiance.[37]

- In a 2018 Gallup poll, only 67% of Americans considered themselves to be Protestant, Catholic, or just generally Christian.[39]

- Only 50% of Americans claimed membership in a church in 2018 compared with 70% in 1999.[40]

- During the same period, the percentage of Americans claiming no religion rose from 8% to 20%. [41]

- A Pew Research Poll in 2018 and 2019 showed only 65% of Americans claiming to be Christians while 26% described themselves as "atheist, agnostic or 'nothing in particular.'"[42]

Not only are there fewer Christians in America, but values are changing even among Christians. In its 2014 Religious Landscape Study, the Pew Research Center found:

- Only 38% of Christians believed there are "clear standards for what is right and wrong" compared with 59% who thought what is right or wrong "depends on the situation;"

- Half of all Christians still believed abortions should be illegal in all or most situations, but the number of Christians accepting of homosexuality increased since 2007 from 44% to 54%—with 44% favoring the legality of same-sex marriage;

- Half of all Christians polled in 2014 also believed in evolution either by natural means (21%) or by God's design (29%).[43]

Conclusion

Yes, much has changed in the United States since 2004 when the Supreme Court refused to rule on the constitutionality of the words "under God" in the Pledge of

Allegiance. The pendulum of public opinion and political influence has swung back and forth between support for or against religious freedom and Christian values. It is likely to keep swinging. But overall, the dominance that Christianity has always held in America as a social and political force is slipping away.

The Supreme Court has affirmed that the government may not show hostility toward religion, but that hasn't stopped many people in the country from calling Christianity a hate group. As a people, we have become more pluralistic than ever before and more polarized about the role of religion in the public sphere. Some promote the beliefs of atheism and the values of humanism while others fight for a return to the Christian values that once characterized us as a nation. Still others believe religion is best left as a private matter where each person is free to believe what they wish, as long as their actions don't diminish the dignity of others.

In Chapter Five, I discussed the three options the Court has considered in reaching its decisions on Establishment Clause issues. When asked to choose between allowing the promotion of Christian beliefs by government agencies or completely removing religious references from the public sphere, the Court has compromised by allowing the government to employ religious traditions which have been largely stripped of their religious meaning by time or context. That includes a reference to God in the Pledge of Allegiance still recited by millions of school children and adults across the country today.

As Christians, we must also consider the options available to us. We can continue to fight to have our government promote our beliefs and values through public prayers, religious monuments, and a deference to the Bible in matters of public policy. We can fight for religious liberty, battling for the right to act according to our religious values even if they conflict with the less religious beliefs of a growing number of Americans. We can attempt to bridge the gap between ourselves and our non-religious neighbors by becoming more accepting of values we once opposed. We can keep our heads down and our mouths shut and keep our religious views to ourselves. Or we can back away from the political and legal fights and focus our attention on proclaiming the gospel to people who need Jesus, not moral laws or the ceremonial religious trappings of a bygone era.

Nearly 80 years ago, a few students were expelled from public school and threatened with incarceration for refusing to pledge their allegiance to the American flag. They agreed with the sentiments of Justice Rehnquist in the quote that opens this chapter that the pledge is a promise of loyalty and allegiance to our nation, and they argued that it violated their religious beliefs to give their allegiance to anyone or anything but God. Not all Christians would agree with their conclusion, even after careful consideration. But what we should all agree on is that our first allegiance must be to God. Everything else we choose to do as Christians must start there.

"You shall have no other gods before me," says the Lord our God (Exodus 20:3). That includes nations, presidents, political parties, our comforts, our families, our freedoms, other people's opinions, and our own safety. The moment we start thinking of any of those things as more important than God, we will be fighting the wrong battles and we may find ourselves on the wrong side of the divide.

~ ~ ~

Appendix A

City upon A Hill
John Winthrop ~1630

Now the onely way to avoyde this shipwracke and to provide for our posterity is to followe the Counsell of Micah, to doe Justly, to love mercy, to walke humbly with our God, for this end, wee must be knitt together in this worke as one man, wee must entertaine each other in brotherly Affeccion, wee must be willing to abridge our selves of our superfluities, for the supply of others necessities, wee must uphold a familiar Commerce together in all meekenes, gentlenes, patience and liberallity, wee must delight in eache other, make others Condicions our owne, rejoyce together, mourne together, labour, and suffer together, allwayes haveing before our eyes our Commission and Community in the worke, our Community as members of the same body, soe shall wee keepe the unitie of the spirit in the bond of peace, the Lord will be our God and delight to dwell among us, as his owne people and will commaund a blessing upon us in all our wayes, soe that wee shall see much more of his wisdome power goodnes and truthe then formerly wee have beene acquainted with, wee shall finde that the God of Israell is among us, when tenn of us shall be able to resist a thousand of our enemies, when hee shall make us a prayse and glory, that men shall say of succeeding plantacions: the lord make it like that of New England: for wee must Consider that wee shall be as a Citty upon a Hill, the eies of all people are uppon us; soe that if wee shall deale falsely with our god in this worke wee have undertaken and soe cause him to withdrawe his present help from us, wee shall be made a story and a byword through the world, wee shall open the mouthes of enemies to speake evill of the wayes of god and all professours for Gods sake; wee shall shame the faces of many of gods worthy servants, and cause theire prayers to be turned into Cursses upon us till wee be consumed out of the good land whether wee are going: And to shutt upp this discourse with that exhortacion of Moses that faithfull servant of the Lord in his last farewell to Israell Deut. 30. Beloved there is now sett before us life, and good, deathe and evill in that wee are Commaunded this day to love the Lord our God, and to love one another to walke in his wayes and to keepe his Commaundements and his Ordinance, and his lawes, and the Articles of our Covenant with him that wee may live and be multiplyed, and that the Lord our God may blesse us in the land whether wee goe to possesse it: But if our heartes shall turne away soe that wee will not obey, but shall be seduced and worshipp other Gods, our pleasures, and proffitts, and serve them, it is propounded unto us this day, wee shall surely perishe out of the good Land whether wee passe over this vast Sea to possesse it;

Therefore lett us choose life, that wee, and our Seede, may live; by obeyeing his voyce, and cleaveing to him, for hee is our life, and our prosperity.

Appendix B

Memorial and Remonstrance
Against Religious Assessments
James Madison ~ 1785

To the Honorable the General Assembly of the Commonwealth of Virginia.

A Memorial and Remonstrance.

We, the subscribers, citizens of the said Commonwealth, having taken into serious consideration, a Bill printed by order of the last Session of General Assembly, entitled 'A Bill establishing a provision for teachers of the Christian Religion,' and conceiving that the same, if finally armed with the sanctions of a law, will be a dangerous abuse of power, are bound as faithful members of a free State, to remonstrate against it, and to declare the reasons by which we are determined. We remonstrate against the said Bill,

1. Because we hold it for a fundamental and undeniable truth, 'that religion, or the duty which we owe to our Creator, and the manner of

discharging it, can be directed only by reason and conviction, not by force or violence.' The Religion then of every man must be left to the conviction and conscience of every man; and it is the right of every man to exercise it as these may dictate. This right is in its nature an unalienable right. It is unalienable; because the opinions of men, depending only on the evidence contemplated by their own minds, cannot follow the dictates of other men: It is unalienable also; because what is here a right towards men, is a duty towards the Creator. It is the duty of every man to render to the Creator such homage, and such only, as he believes to be acceptable to him. This duty is predecent, both in order of time and degree of obligation, to the claims of Civil Society. Before any man can be considered as a member of Civil Society, he must be considered as a subject of the Governor of the Universe: And if a member of Civil Society, who enters into any subordinate Association, must always do it with a reservation of his duty to the general authority; much more must every man who becomes a member of any particular Civil Society, do it with a saving of his allegiance to the Universal Sovereign. We maintain therefore that in matters of Religion, no man's right is abridged by the institution of Civil Society, and that Religion is wholly exempt from its cognizance. True it is, that no other rule exists, by which any question which may divide a Society, can be ultimately determined, but the will of the majority; but it is also true, that the majority may trespass on the rights of the minority.

2. Because if religion be exempt from the authority of the Society at large, still less can it be subject to that of the Legislative Body. The latter are but the creatures and vicegerents of the former. Their jurisdiction is both derivative and limited: it is limited with regard to the co-ordinate departments, more necessarily is it limited with regard to the constituents. The preservation of a free government requires not merely, that the metes

and bounds which separate each department of power may be invariably maintained; but, more especially, that neither of them be suffered to overleap the great Barrier which defends the rights of the people. The Rulers who are guilty of such an encroachment, exceed the commission from which they derive their authority, and are Tyrants. The People who submit to it are governed by laws made neither by themselves, nor by an authority derived from them, and are slaves.

3. Because, it is proper to take alarm at the first experiment on our liberties. We hold this prudent jealousy to be the first duty of citizens, and one of (the) noblest characteristics of the late Revolution. The freemen of America did not wait till usurped power had strengthened itself by exercise, and entangled the question in precedents. They saw all the consequences in the principle, and they avoided the consequences by denying the principle. We revere this lesson too much, soon to forget it. Who does not see that the same authority which can establish Christianity, in exclusion of all other Religions, may establish with the same ease any particular sect of Christians, in exclusion of all other Sects? That the same authority which can force a citizen to contribute three pence only of his property for the support of any one establishment, may force him to conform to any other establishment in all cases whatsoever?

4. Because, the bill violates that equality which ought to be the basis of every law, and which is more indispensable, in proportion as the validity or expediency of any law is more liable to be impeached. If 'all men are by nature equally free and independent,' all men are to be considered as entering into Society on equal conditions; as relinquishing no more, and therefore retaining no less, one than another, of their natural rights. Above all are they to be considered as retaining an 'equal title to the free exercise of Religion according to the dictates of conscience'. Whilst we

assert for ourselves a freedom to embrace, to profess and to observe the Religion which we believe to be of divine origin, we cannot deny an equal freedom to those whose minds have not yet yielded to the evidence which has convinced us. If this freedom be abused, it is an offence against God, not against man: To God, therefore, not to men, must an account of it be rendered. As the bill violates equality by subjecting some to peculiar burdens; so it violates the same principle, by granting to others peculiar exemptions. Are the Quakers and Menonists the only sects who think a compulsive support of their religions unnecessary and unwarrantable? Can their piety alone be intrusted with the care of public worship? Ought their Religions to be endowed above all others, with extraordinary privileges, by which proselytes may be enticed from all others? We think too favorably of the justice and good sense of these denominations, to believe that they either covet pre-eminencies over their fellow citizens, or that they will be seduced by them, from the common opposition to the measure.

5. Because the bill implies either that the Civil Magistrate is a competent Judge of Religious truth; or that he may employ Religion as an engine of Civil policy. The first is an arrogant pretension falsified by the contradictory opinions of Rulers in all ages, and throughout the world: The second an unhallowed perversion of the means of salvation.

6. Because the establishment proposed by the Bill is not requisite for the support of the Christian Religion. To say that it is, is a contradiction to the Christian Religion itself; for every page of it disavows a dependence on the powers of this world: it is a contradiction to fact; for it is known that this Religion both existed and flourished, not only without the support of human laws, but in spite of every opposition from them; and not only during the period of miraculous aid, but long after it had been left to its own evidence, and the ordinary care of Providence: Nay, it is a

contradiction in terms; for a Religion not invented by human policy, must have pre-existed and been supported, before it was established by human policy. It is moreover to weaken in those who profess this Religion a pious confidence in its innate excellence, and the patronage of its Author; and to foster in those who still reject it, a suspicion that its friends are too conscious of its fallacies, to trust it to its own merits.

7. Because experience witnesseth that ecclesiastical establishments, instead of maintaining the purity and efficacy of Religion, have had a contrary operation. During almost fifteen centuries, has the legal establishment of Christianity been on trial. What have been its fruits? More or less in all places, pride and indolence in the Clergy; ignorance and servility in the laity; in both, superstition, bigotry and persecution. Enquire of the Teachers of Christianity for the ages in which it appeared in its greatest lustre; those of every sect, point to the ages prior to its incorporation with Civil policy. Propose a restoration of this primitive state in which its Teachers depended on the voluntary rewards of their flocks; many of them predict its downfall. On which side ought their testimony to have greatest weight, when for or when against their interest?

8. Because the establishment in question is not necessary for the support of Civil Government. If it be urged as necessary for the support of Civil Government only as it is a means of supporting Religion, and it be not necessary for the latter purpose, it cannot be necessary for the former. If Religion be not within (the) cognizance of Civil Government, how can its legal establishment be said to be necessary to Civil Government? What influence in fact have ecclesiastical establishments had on Civil Society? In some instances they have been seen to erect a spiritual tyranny on the ruins of Civil authority; in many instances they have been seen upholding the thrones of political tyranny; in no instance have they been seen the

guardians of the liberties of the people. Rulers who wished to subvert the public liberties, may have found an established clergy convenient auxiliaries. A just government, instituted to secure & perpetuate it, needs them not. Such a government will be best supported by protecting every citizen in the enjoyment of his Religion with the same equal hand which protects his person and his property; by neither invading the equal rights by any Sect, nor suffering any Sect to invade those of another.

9. Because the proposed establishment is a departure from that generous policy, which, offering an asylum to the persecuted and oppressed of every Nation and Religion, promised a lustre to our country, and an accession to the number of its citizens. What a melancholy mark is the Bill of sudden degeneracy? Instead of holding forth an asylum to the persecuted, it is itself a signal of persecution. It degrades from the equal rank of Citizens all those whose opinions in Religion do not bend to those of the Legislative authority. Distant as it may be, in its present form, from the Inquisition it differs from it only in degree. The one is the first step, the other the last in the career of intolerance. The magnanimous sufferer under this cruel scourge in foreign Regions, must view the Bill as a Beacon on our Coast, warning him to seek some other haven, where liberty and philanthropy in their due extent may offer a more certain repose from his troubles.

10. Because, it will have a like tendency to banish our Citizens. The allurements presented by other situations are every day thinning their number. To superadd a fresh motive to emigration, by revoking the liberty which they now enjoy, would be the same species of folly which has dishonoured and depopulated flourishing kingdoms.

11. Because, it will destroy that moderation and harmony which the forbearance of our laws to intermeddle with Religion, has produced

amongst its several sects. Torrents of blood have been spilt in the old world, by vain attempts of the secular arm to extinguish Religious discord, by proscribing all difference in Religious opinions. Time has at length revealed the true remedy. Every relaxation of narrow and rigorous policy, wherever it has been tried, has been found to assuage the disease. The American Theatre has exhibited proofs, that equal and complete liberty, if it does not wholly eradicate it, sufficiently destroys its malignant influence on the health and prosperity of the State. If with the salutary effects of this system under our own eyes, we begin to contract the bonds of Religious freedom, we know no name that will too severely reproach our folly. At least let warning be taken at the first fruit of the threatened innovation. The very appearance of the Bill has transformed that 'Christian forbearance, love and charity,' which of late mutually prevailed, into animosities and jealousies, which may not soon be appeased. What mischiefs may not be dreaded should this enemy to the public quiet be armed with the force of a law?

12. Because, the policy of the bill is adverse to the diffusion of the light of Christianity. The first wish of those who enjoy this precious gift, ought to be that it may be imparted to the whole race of mankind. Compare the number of those who have as yet received it with the number still remaining under the dominion of false Religions; and how small is the former! Does the policy of the Bill tend to lessen the disproportion? No; it at once discourages those who are strangers to the light of (revelation) from coming into the Region of it; and countenances, by example the nations who continue in darkness, in shutting out those who might convey it to them. Instead of levelling as far as possible, every obstacle to the victorious progress of truth, the Bill with an ignoble and unchristian

timidity would circumscribe it, with a wall of defence, against the encroachments of error.

13. Because attempts to enforce by legal sanctions, acts obnoxious to so great a proportion of Citizens, tend to enervate the laws in general, and to slacken the bands of Society. If it be difficult to execute any law which is not generally deemed necessary or salutary, what must be the case where it is deemed invalid and dangerous? and what may be the effect of so striking an example of impotency in the Government, on its general authority?

14. Because a measure of such singular magnitude and delicacy ought not to be imposed, without the clearest evidence that it is called for by a majority of citizens: and no satisfactory method is yet proposed by which the voice of the majority in this case may be determined, or its influence secured. 'The people of the respective counties are indeed requested to signify their opinion respecting the adoption of the Bill to the next Session of Assembly.' But the representation must be made equal, before the voice either of the Representatives or of the Counties, will be that of the people. Our hope is that neither of the former will, after due consideration, expouse the dangerous principle of the Bill. Should the event disappoint us, it will still leave us in full confidence, that a fair appeal to the latter will reverse the sentence against our liberties.

15. Because, finally, 'the equal right of every citizen to the free exercise of his Religion according to the dictates of conscience' is held by the same tenure with all our other rights. If we recur to its origin, it is equally the gift of nature; if we weigh its importance, it cannot be less dear to us; if we consult the Declaration of those rights which pertain to the good people of Virginia, as the 'basis and foundation of Government,' it is enumerated with equal solemnity, or rather studied emphasis. Either

then, we must say, that the will of the Legislature is the only measure of their authority; and that in the plentitude of this authority, they may sweep away all our fundamental rights; or, that they are bound to leave this particular right untouched and sacred: Either we must say, that they may controul the freedom of the press, may abolish the trial by jury, may swallow up the Executive and Judiciary Powers of the State; nay that they may despoil us of our very right of suffrage, and erect themselves into an independent and hereditary assembly: or we must say, that they have no authority to enact into law the Bill under consideration. We the subscribers say, that the General Assembly of this Commonwealth have no such authority: And that no effort may be omitted on our part, against so dangerous an usurpation, we oppose to it, this remonstrance; earnestly praying, as we are in duty bound, that the Supreme Lawgiver of the Universe, by illuminating those to whom it is addressed, may on the one hand, turn their councils from every act which would affront his holy prerogative, or violate the trust committed to them: and on the other, guide them into every measure which may be worthy of his blessing, may redound to their own praise, and may establish more firmly the liberties, the prosperity, and the Happiness of the Commonwealth.

Appendix C

Excerpts of U.S. Supreme Court case
Engle v. Vitale
1962

Mr. Justice Black delivered the opinion of the Court.

The respondent Board of Education...directed the School District's principal to cause the following prayer to be said aloud by each class in the presence of a teacher at the beginning of each school day: "Almighty God, we acknowledge our dependence upon Thee, and we beg Thy blessings upon us, our parents, our teachers and our Country."

This daily procedure was adopted on the recommendation of the State Board of Regents, a governmental agency created by the State Constitution to which the New York Legislature has granted broad supervisory, executive, and legislative powers over the State's public school system. These state officials composed the prayer which they recommended and published as a part of their "Statement on Moral and Spiritual Training in the Schools," saying: "We believe that this Statement will be subscribed to by all men and women of good will, and we call upon all of them to aid in giving life to our program."

Shortly after the practice of reciting the Regents' prayer was adopted by the School District, the parents of ten pupils brought this action.... The petitioners contend among other things that the state laws requiring or permitting use of the Regents' prayer must be struck down as a violation of the Establishment Clause because that prayer was composed by governmental officials as a part of a governmental program to further religious beliefs. For this reason, petitioners argue, the State's use of the Regents' prayer in its public school system breaches the constitutional wall of separation between Church and State. We agree with that contention since we think that the constitutional prohibition against laws respecting an establishment of religion must at least mean that in this country it is no part of the business of government to compose official prayers for any group of the American people to recite as a part of a religious program carried on by government.

It is a matter of history that this very practice of establishing governmentally composed prayers for religious services was one of the reasons which caused many of our early colonists to leave England and seek religious freedom in America. The Book of Common Prayer, which was created under governmental direction and which was approved by Acts of Parliament in 1548 and 1549, set out in minute detail the accepted form and content of prayer and other religious ceremonies to be used in the established, tax-supported Church of England. The controversies over the Book and what should be its content repeatedly threatened to disrupt the peace of that country as the accepted forms of prayer in the established church changed with the views of the particular ruler that happened to be in control at the time. Powerful groups representing some of the varying religious views of the people struggled among themselves to impress their particular views upon the Government and obtain amendments of the Book more suitable to their respective notions of how religious services should be conducted in order that the official religious establishment would advance their particular religious beliefs. Other groups, lacking the necessary political power to influence the Government on the matter, decided to leave England and its established church and seek freedom in America from England's governmentally ordained and supported religion.

It is an unfortunate fact of history that when some of the very groups which had most strenuously opposed the established Church of England found themselves sufficiently in control of colonial governments in this country to write their own prayers into law, they passed laws making their own religion the official religion of their respective colonies. Indeed, as late as the time of the Revolutionary War, there were established churches in at least eight of the thirteen former colonies and established religions in at least four of the other five. But the successful Revolution against English political domination was shortly followed by intense opposition to the practice of establishing religion by law. This opposition crystallized rapidly into an effective political force in Virginia where the minority religious groups such as Presbyterians, Lutherans, Quakers and Baptists had gained such strength that the adherents to the established Episcopal Church were actually a minority themselves. In 1785-1786, those opposed to the established Church, led by James Madison and Thomas Jefferson, who, though themselves not members of any of these dissenting religious groups, opposed all religious establishments by law on grounds of principle, obtained the enactment of the famous "Virginia Bill for Religious Liberty" by which all religious groups were placed on an equal footing so far as the State was concerned. Similar though less far-reaching legislation was being considered and passed in other States.

By the time of the adoption of the Constitution, our history shows that there was a widespread awareness among many Americans of the dangers of a union of Church and State. These people knew, some of them from bitter personal experience, that one of the greatest dangers to the freedom of the individual to worship in his own way lay in the Government's placing its official stamp of approval upon one particular kind of prayer or one particular form of religious services. They knew the anguish, hardship and bitter strife that could come when zealous religious groups struggled with one another to obtain the Government's stamp of approval from each King, Queen, or Protector that came to temporary power. The Constitution was intended to avert a part of this danger by leaving the government of this country in the hands of the people rather than in the hands of any monarch. But this safeguard was not enough. Our Founders were no more willing to let the content of their prayers and their privilege of praying whenever they pleased be influenced by the ballot box than they were to let these vital matters of personal conscience depend upon the succession of monarchs. The First Amendment was added to the Constitution to stand as a guarantee that neither the power nor the prestige of the Federal Government would be used to control, support or influence the kinds of prayer the American people can say—that the people's religions must not be subjected to the pressures of government for change each time a new political administration is elected to office. Under that Amendment's prohibition against governmental establishment of religion, as reinforced by the provisions of the Fourteenth Amendment, government in this country, be it state or federal, is without power to prescribe by law any particular form of prayer which is to be used as an official prayer in carrying on any program of governmentally sponsored religious activity….

When the power, prestige and financial support of government is placed behind a particular religious belief, the indirect coercive pressure upon religious minorities to conform to the prevailing officially approved religion is plain. But the purposes underlying the Establishment Clause go much further than that. Its first and most immediate purpose rested on the belief that a union of government and religion tends to destroy government and to degrade religion. The history of governmentally established religion, both in England and in this country, showed that whenever government had allied itself with one particular form of religion, the inevitable result had been that it had incurred the hatred, disrespect and even contempt of those who held contrary beliefs. That same history showed that many people had lost their respect for any religion that had relied upon the support of government to spread its faith. The Establishment Clause thus stands as an expression of principle on the part of the Founders of our Constitution that religion is too personal, too sacred, too holy, to permit its "unhallowed perversion" by a civil magistrate. Another purpose of the Establishment Clause rested upon an awareness of the historical fact that governmentally established religions and religious persecutions go hand in hand. The Founders knew that only a few years after the Book of Common Prayer became the only accepted form of religious services in the established Church of England, an Act of Uniformity was passed to compel all Englishmen to attend those services and to make it a criminal offense to conduct or attend religious gatherings of any other kind—a law which was consistently flouted by dissenting religious groups in England and which contributed to widespread persecutions of people like John Bunyan who persisted in holding "unlawful [religious] meetings. . .to the great disturbance and distraction of the good subjects of this kingdom. . . ." And they knew that similar persecutions had received the sanction of law in several of the colonies in this country soon after the establishment of official religions in those colonies. It was in large part to get completely away from this sort of systematic religious persecution that the Founders brought into being our Nation, our Constitution, and our Bill of Rights with its prohibition against any governmental establishment of religion. The New York laws officially prescribing the Regents' prayer are inconsistent both with the purposes of the Establishment Clause and with the Establishment Clause itself.

It has been argued that to apply the Constitution in such a way as to prohibit state laws respecting an establishment of religious services in public schools is to indicate a hostility toward religion or toward prayer. Nothing, of course, could be more wrong. The history of man is inseparable from the history of religion. And perhaps it is not too much to say that since the beginning of that history many people have devoutly believed that "More things are wrought by prayer than this world dreams of." It was doubtless largely due to men who believed this that there grew up a sentiment that caused men to leave the cross-currents of officially established state religions and religious persecution in Europe and come to this country filled with the hope that they could find a place in which they could pray when they pleased to the God of their faith in the language they chose. And there were men of this same faith in the power of prayer who led the fight for adoption of our Constitution and also for our Bill of Rights with the very guarantees of religious freedom that forbid the sort of governmental activity which New York has attempted here. These men knew that the First Amendment, which tried to put an end to governmental control of religion and of prayer, was not written to destroy either. They knew rather that it was written to quiet well-justified fears which nearly all of them felt arising out of an awareness that governments of the past had shackled men's tongues to make them speak only the religious thoughts that government wanted them to speak and to pray only to the God that government wanted them to pray to. It is neither sacrilegious nor antireligious to say that each separate government in this country should stay out of the business of writing or sanctioning official prayers and leave that purely religious function to the people themselves and to those the people choose to look to for religious guidance.

It is true that New York's establishment of its Regents' prayer as an officially approved religious doctrine of that State does not amount to a total establishment of one particular religious sect to the exclusion of all others—that, indeed, the governmental endorsement of that prayer seems relatively insignificant when compared to the governmental encroachments upon religion which were commonplace 200 years ago. To those who may subscribe to the view that because the Regents' official prayer is so brief and general there can be no danger to religious freedom in its governmental establishment, however, it may be appropriate to say in the words of James Madison, the author of the First Amendment:

"[I]t is proper to take alarm at the first experiment on our liberties. . . . Who does not see that the same authority which can establish Christianity, in exclusion of all other Religions, may establish with the same ease any particular sect of Christians, in exclusion of all other Sects? That the same authority which can force a citizen to contribute three pence only of his property for the support of any one establishment, may force him to conform to any other establishment in all cases whatsoever?"

The judgment of the Court of Appeals of New York is reversed and the cause remanded for further proceedings not inconsistent with this opinion.

Reversed and remanded.

Mr. Justice Stewart, dissenting.

A local school board in New York has provided that those pupils who wish to do so may join in a brief prayer at the beginning of each school day, acknowledging their dependence upon God and asking His blessing upon them and upon their parents, their teachers, and their country. The Court today decides that in permitting this brief nondenominational prayer the school board has violated the Constitution of the United States. I think this decision is wrong....

With all respect, I think the Court has misapplied a great constitutional principle. I cannot see how an "official religion" is established by letting those who want to say a prayer say it. On the contrary, I think that to deny the wish of these school children to join in reciting this prayer is to deny them the opportunity of sharing in the spiritual heritage of our Nation.

The Court's historical review of the quarrels over the Book of Common Prayer in England throws no light for me on the issue before us in this case. England had then and has now an established church. Equally unenlightening, I think, is the history of the early establishment and later rejection of an official church in our own States. For we deal here not with the establishment of a state church, which would, of course, be constitutionally impermissible, but with whether school children who want to begin their day by joining in prayer must be prohibited from doing so. Moreover, I think that the Court's task, in this as in all areas of constitutional adjudication, is not responsibly aided by the uncritical invocation of metaphors like the "wall of separation," a phrase nowhere to be found in the Constitution. What is relevant to the issue here is not the history of an established church in sixteenth century England or in eighteenth century America, but the history of the religious traditions of our people, reflected in countless practices of the institutions and officials of our government.

At the opening of each day's Session of this Court we stand, while one of our officials invokes the protection of God. Since the days of John Marshall our Crier has said, "God save the United States and this Honorable Court." Both the Senate and the House of Representatives open their daily Sessions with prayer. Each of our Presidents, from George Washington to John F. Kennedy, has upon assuming his Office asked the protection and help of God.

The Court today says that the state and federal governments are without constitutional power to prescribe any particular form of words to be recited by any group of the American people on any subject touching religion. One of the stanzas of "The Star-Spangled Banner," made our National Anthem by Act of Congress in 1931, contains these verses:

"Blest with victory and peace, may the heav'n rescued land

Praise the Pow'r that hath made and preserved us a nation!

Then conquer we must, when our cause it is just,

And this be our motto 'In God is our Trust.'"

In 1954 Congress added a phrase to the Pledge of Allegiance to the Flag so that it now contains the words "one Nation under God, indivisible, with liberty and justice for all." In 1952 Congress enacted legislation calling upon the President each year to proclaim a National Day of Prayer. Since 1865 the words "IN GOD WE TRUST" have been impressed on our coins.

Countless similar examples could be listed, but there is no need to belabor the obvious. It was all summed up by this Court just ten years ago in a single sentence: "We are a religious people whose institutions presuppose a Supreme Being." *Zorach v. Clauson.*

I do not believe that this Court, or the Congress, or the President has by the actions and practices I have mentioned established an "official religion" in violation of the Constitution. And I do not believe the State of New York has done so in this case. What each has done has been to recognize and to follow the deeply entrenched and highly cherished spiritual traditions of our Nation—traditions which come down to us from those who almost two hundred years ago avowed their "firm Reliance on the Protection of divine Providence" when they proclaimed the freedom and independence of this brave new world.

I dissent.

Chapter Notes

Chapter One

1. *Engel v. Vitale*, 370 U.S. 421 (1962) (daily prayer recited by students violates Establishment Clause); *Lee V. Weisman*, 505 U.S. 577 (1992) (prayer at public school graduation violates Establishment Clause).

2. *Glassroth v. Moore*, No. 021678pv2 (11th Cir., Oct. 11, 2003).

3. *Allegheny County v. Greater Pittsburgh ACLU*, 492 U.S. 573 (1989).

4. Debra Rosenberg, "Protest and Prayer," *Newsweek*, March 24, 2004.

5. Id.

6. *Elk Grove Unified School District v. Newdow*, 542 U.S. 1 (2004)

7. *Newdow v. United States Congress*, 328 F.3d 466 (9th Cir. 2003). The court recognized Newdow's standing to complain about the practices of Elk Grove Unified School District, where his daughter was a student, but not the practices of Sacramento City Unified School District. This effectively dismissed Sacramento City Unified School District and its superintendent from the case.

8. U.S. Constitution, Art. I, sec. 6, clause 1.

9. *Newdow*, supra.

10. Charles Lane, "U.S. Court Votes to Bar Pledge of Allegiance; Use of 'God' Called Unconstitutional," *The Washington Post*, June 27, 2002; and Maura Dolan, "Pledge of Allegiance Violates Constitution, Court Declares," *Los Angeles Times*, June 27, 2002.

11. Scott Gold and Eric Bailey, "1 Plaintiff, Against the Grain," *Los Angeles Times*, June 27, 2002.

12. Scott Gold, "Keep God in the Pledge, an Angry Chorus Cries," *Los Angeles Times*, June 28, 2002.

13. Howard Fineman, et al., "One Nation, Under… Who?" *Newsweek*, July 8, 2002.

14. Debra Rosenberg, "Protest and Prayer," *Newsweek*, March 24, 2004; Charles Lane, "Justices Keep 'Under God' in Pledge," *Washington Post*, June 15, 2004.

15. Rev. David A. Highfield, Westminster, Md., letter to the editor, *Newsweek*, July 22, 2002.

16. *Newdow*, supra.

17. Id. Three of the justices wanted to overturn the Ninth Circuit's decision by finding the wording of the Pledge constitutional. The opinions of these Justices will be examined in Chapter Four.

18. Id.

19. Id.

Chapter Two

1. *Everson v. Board of Education of Ewing Township*, 330 U.S. 1, 9-10 (1947) (citing Cobb, *Religious Liberty in America*, 1902, and other sources); *Engel v. Vitale*, 370 U.S. 421, 428 (1962).

2. *Engle*, 370 U.S. at 428; also *Everson*, 330 U.S. at 14.

3. M.E. Bradford, *A Worthy Company* (Marlborough, NH: Plymouth Rock Foundation, 1982), p. viii; and Michael Novak, *On Two Wings: Humble Faith and Common Sense at the American Founding* (San Francisco: Encounter Books, 2003), p 147.

4. Joseph Story, *Commentaries on the Constitution of the United States*, Vol. 3, p. 1873 (1833).

5. U.S. Constitution, Art. VI, para. 3.

6. *Wallace v. Jaffree*, 472 U.S. 38, 93 (1985) (citing J. Elliot, Debates on the Federal Constitution (1891).

7. *Jaffree*, 472 U.S. at 94.

8. *Jaffree*, 472 U.S. at 97.

9. 1 Annals of Congress 730 (August 15, 1789).

10. *Jaffree*, 472 U.S. at 95.

11. *Everson*, 330 U.S. at 11-12, 35.

12. Madison, "Memorial and Remonstrance Against Religious Assessments," para. 1.

13. Letter to Edward Livingston from James Madison, 1822, quoted in Novak, *On Two Wings*, supra, p. 57-58.

14. Alison Weir, *The Children of Henry VIII* (New York: Ballantine Books, 1996), p. 296; and B. K. Kuiper, *The Church in History* (Grand Rapids: CSI Publications, 2002), pp. 228-29, 254-57.

15. *Everson*, 330 U.S. at 8-9.

16. The Virginia Declaration of Rights, 1776, paragraph 16, quoted in Jerome B. Agel., *We, The People: Great Documents of the American Nation* (New York: Barnes & Noble Books, 2000), p. 15-16.

17. The Northwest Ordinance, 1 Stat. 50, 52, n. (a), quoted in Agel, *We The People*, p. 73-77.

18. 1 Annals of Cong. 914 (1789). John Adams and James Madison also issued Thanksgiving Day Proclamations which were prompted by Congress, and in 1941 Congress officially made Thanksgiving Day a national holiday.

19. J. Richardson, *Messages and Papers of the Presidents, 1789-1897*, (1897) Vol. 1, p. 64.

20. George Washington, "Washington's Farewell Address 1796," quoted in Agel, *We The People*, p. 276-278.

21. John Adams, "To the Officers of the First Brigade of the Third Division of the Militia of Massachusetts, October 11, 1798," quoted in Bennett, *Our Sacred Honor* (New York: Simon & Shuster, 1997), p. 370.

22. Thomas Jefferson, "Notes on the State of Virginia," in Merrill D. Peterson, *Thomas Jefferson: Writings* (New York: Library of America, 1984), Query XVIII, p. 289.

23. The Declaration of Independence, 1776, paragraph 2, quoted in Agel, *We The People*, p. 17-20.

24. Madison, "Memorial and Remonstrance," para. 1.

25. Madison., para. 4.

26. Madison, para. 3.

Chapter Three

1. Benjamin Franklin in a letter to Jean Baptiste Le Roy, November 13, 1789, quoted in Shrager and Frost, eds., *The Quotable Lawyer* (New York: Facts on File 1986), p. 56.

2. *Walz. v. Tax Comm'n*, 397 U.S. 664, 694 (1970) (opinion of Harlan, J.).

3. United States Constitution, Amendment 14, Section 1 (1868).

4. Id., Section 5.

5. *Gitlow v. New York*, 268 U.S. 652, 666 (1925).

6. *Cantwell v. State of Connecticut*, 310 U.S. 296 (1940).

7. Id.

8. *Reynold v. United States*, 98 U.S. 145 (1879) (jurisdiction in this case was based on federal authority of the U.S. Territories, and not on the Fourteenth Amendment).

9. *Cantwell*, 310 U.S. at 303.

10. *Reynolds*, 98 U.S. at 166.

11. *Reynolds*, 98 U.S. at 164 (quoting 8 *Writings of Thomas Jefferson* 113 (H. Washington ed. 1861) (Jefferson's letter to the Danbury Baptist Association)).

12. *Reynolds*, 98 U.S. at 164.

13. States may apply child labor laws to prohibit children from selling religious books door-to-door. *Prince v. Commonwealth of Massachusetts*, 321 U.S. 158 (1944). Cities may require a permit for the use of a public park for a religious meeting if the permitting system is non-discriminatory. *Poulos v. New Hampshire*, 345 U.S. 395 (1953). The Air Force may prohibit an orthodox Jew from wearing indoors the yarmulke required by his faith. *Goldman v. Weinberger*, 475 U.S. 503 (1986). Social security taxes must be paid by Amish employers, even though such a payment is against their religious beliefs. *United States v. Lee*, 455 U.S. 252 (1982). And states may prohibit the use of hallucinogenic drugs, even if one such drug is used in the religious ceremonies of some Native Americans. *Employment Division v. Smith*, 494 U.S. 872 (1990).

14. States may not deny unemployment benefits simply because a person refuses to accept work contrary to his religious beliefs, *Sherbert v. Verner*, 374 U.S. 398 (1963), or interfere with the right of parents to direct the education of their children, *Pierce v. Society of Sisters*, 268 U.S. 510 (1925), or apply compulsory school-attendance laws against Amish parents who refused on religious grounds to send their children to school, *Wisconsin v. Yoder*, 406 U.S. 205 (1972). Nor may individuals be compelled to express beliefs contrary to their religious convictions. *Wooley v. Maynard*, 430 U.S. 705 (1977) (invalidating compelled display of a license plate slogan); *West Virginia State Board of Education v. Barnette*, 319 U.S. 624, 629 (1943) (invalidating requirement that all public school students recite Pledge of Allegiance). Finally, laws may not be written to target a specific religious practice, such as making the killing of animals in religious rituals illegal, although the killing of animals in general was not proscribed. *Church of Lukumi Babalu Aye, Inc. v. City of Hialeah*, 124 L.Ed. 2d 472 (1993).

15. *Employment Division v. Smith*, 494 U.S. 872 (1990).

16. *Everson v. Board of Education of Ewing Township*, 330 U.S. 1 (1947).

17. *Everson*, 330 U.S. at 18.

18. *Everson*, 330 U.S. at 15-16 (quoting in the last sentence *Reynold v. United States*, 98 U.S. 145, 164 (1878).

19. *Wallace v. Jaffree*, 472 U.S. 38, 107 (1985) (Justice Rehnquist, dissenting) (internal citations deleted).

20. *Illinois ex re. McCollum*, 333 U.S. 203 (1948).

21. *Zorach v. Clauson*, 343 U.S. 306 (1952).

22. *Zorach*, 343 U.S. at 313-14.

23. *Engel v. Vitale*, 370 U.S. 421 (1962).

24. *Abington School District v. Schempp*, 374 U.S. 203 (1963).

25. *Stone v. Graham*, 449 U.S. 39 (1980).

26. *Wallace*, 472 U.S. 38.

27. *Lee v. Weisman*, 505 U.S. 577 (1992).

28. *Widmar v. Vincent*, 454 U.S. 263 (1981).

29. *Westside Community Board of Education v. Mergens*, 496 U.S. 226 (1990).

30. *Lamb's Chapel v. Center Moriches School District*, 508 U.S. 384 (1993).

31. *Capitol Square Review Bd. v. Pinette* 115 S. Ct. 2440 (1995).

32. *Allegheny County v. Greater Pittsburgh ACLU*, 492 U.S. 573 (1989).

33. *Lynch v. Donnelly*, 465 U.S. 668 (1984).

34. *Marsh v. Chambers*, 463 U.S. 783 (1983).

35. *Marsh*, 463 U.S. at 787.

36. *Marsh*, 463 U.S. at 796 (Justice Brennan, dissenting).

37. *Engle*, 370 U.S. at 450 (quoting the last sentence of the Declaration of Independence).

38. Joseph Story, *Commentaries on the Constitution of the United States*, Vol. 2 (5th ed. 1981) p. 630-32.

39. *Engle*, 370 U.S. at 429-430.

Chapter Four

1. Petition for a Writ of Certiorari in *Elk Grove Unified School District v. Newdow*, U.S.S.Ct. No. 02-1624, p. 12.

2. Amicus brief of Texas, et al., in support of petitioners in *Elk Grove Unified School District v. Newdow* U.S.S.Ct. No. 02-1624, p. 2

3. *Minersville School District v. Gobitis*, 310 U.S. 586 (1940).

4. *Gobitis*, 310 U.S. at 595.

5. *Gobitis*, 310 U.S. at 596.

6. *Reynolds v. United States*, 98 U.S. 145 (1879); *United States v. Schwimmer*, 279 U.S. 644 (1929).

7. *West Virginia State Board of Education v. Barnette*, 319 U.S. 624, 629 (1943).

8. *Barnette*, 319 U.S. 614.

9. *Barnette*, 319 U.S. 614.

10. *Reynolds*, 98 U.S. at 164.

11. *Barnette*, 319 U.S. at 630.

12. *Barnette*, 319 U.S. at 642.

13. *Barnette*, 319 U.S. at 644.

14. *Newdow v. United States Congress*, 292 F.3d 597 (9th Cir. 2002).

15. SharpMan.com, *The Care and Display of the American Flag*, (New York: Stewart, Tabori & Chang, 2004); also *The Story of the Pledge of Allegiance*, September 2004 <www.flagday.org/Pages/StoryofPledge.html>.

16. Id.

17. 36 U.S.C. 172 and annotations.

18. 36 U.S.C. 172; also <www.flagday.org/Pages/StoryofPledge.html>.

19. Letter from Dwight D. Eisenhower to Luke E. Hart, Supreme Knight of the Knights of Columbus, Aug. 17, 1954, reprinted in *"Under God" Under Attack*, (Columbia, 2002) and quoted in a brief in support of petitioners by The Knights of Columbus in *Elk Grove v. Newdow*.

20. 100 Congressional Record 5750 (1954).

21. World War II, Causes and Outbreak, Encyclopedia.com 2002, September 2004, <Http://www.encyclopedia.com/html/section/WW2_CausesandOutbreak.asp>.

22. World War II, War Comes to the United States, Encyclopedia.com 2002, September 2004, <Http://www.encyclopedia.com/html/section/WW2_WarComestotheUnited States.asp>.

23. Adolf Hitler, *Mein Kampf* (1924), quoted in Felix Gilbert, *The End of the European Era, 1890 to the Present* (New York: W.W. Norton & Co., 1970), p. 223.

24. *Barnette*, 319 U.S. at 640-41.

Chapter Five

1. Merriam-Webster Online Dictionary, October 2004, <www.m-w.com>.

2. John Winthrop, 1630, quoted by Vincent Ferraro, Mount Holyoke College, *John Winthrop's City upon a Hill, 1630* , September 2004, <http://www.mtholyoke.edu/acad/intrel/winthrop.htm >.

3. *Lemon v. Kurtzman*, 403 U.S. 602, 612-13 (1984).

4. *Lynch v. Donnelly*, 465 U.S. 668 (1984).

5. *Allegheny County v. Greater Pittsburgh ACLU*, 492 U.S. 573 (1989).

6. *Lynch*, 465 U.S. at 692.

7. *Lynch*, 465 U.S. at 692-93.

8. *Lynch*, 465 U.S. at 716-17 (internal citations omitted).

9. Petition for a Writ of Certiorari to the United States Court of Appeals for the Ninth Circuit, *Elk Grove Unified School District v. Newdow*.

10. All quotes in this section are taken from Os Guiness, *The Great Experiment, Faith and Freedom in America* (Colorado Springs: NavPress, 2001) pp. 138-154.

11. Learned Hand, quoted in David Shrager and Elizabeth Frost, eds., *The Quotable Lawyer* (New York: New England Publishing Associates, 1986), p. 60.

12. The Mayflower Compact, 1620, quoted in Agel, *We The People*, p. 4.

13. "You are the light of the world. A city on a hill cannot be hidden." Matthew 5:14

14. Ferraro, *John Winthrop's City upon a Hill, 1630*.

15. James Madison, "Memorial and Remonstrance Against Religious Assessments," par. 1.

16. Letter to Edward Livingston from James Madison, 1822, quoted in Novak, *On Two Wings*, p. 57-58.

Chapter Six

1. John Adams, *Diary*, 1765, quoted in Guiness, *The Great Experiment*, p. 17.

2. Senator Albert J. Beveridge, Speech in the U.S. Senate, 1900, quoted in Guiness, *The Great Experiment*, p. 18.

3. President George W. Bush, June 11, 2004 at President Ronald Reagan's funeral at the National Cathedral (quoted in "George W. Bush: Standing His Ground," by Carl Cannon, *Readers Digest*, August 2004, p. 78.)

Chapter Seven

1. Ferraro, *John Winthrop's City upon a Hill, 1630* , <http://www.mtholyoke.edu/acad/intrel/winthrop.htm >.

2. Hobart Freeman, *An Introduction to the Old Testament Prophets* (Chicago: Moody Press, 1968), p. 163.

3. Freeman, p. 163.

Chapter Eight

1. William Bradford, *Of Plimoth Plantation, 1620-1647*, first published in full in 1856, quoted in Gary D. Schmidt, *William Bradford; Plymouth's Faithful Pilgrim* (Grand Rapids, MI: Eerdmans Books for Young Readers, 1999), p. 51.

2. Bradford.

Chapter Nine

1. *Elk Grove Unified School District v. Newdow, 542 U.S. 1* (2004) (Chief Justice Rehnquist concurring).

2. *Newdow v. Congress of United States*, 383 F. Supp. 2d 1229, 1239 (E.D. Cal. 2005).

3. *Newdow, et al v. Rio Linda Union School Dist., et al,* No. 05-17257 (9th Cir. 2010), p. 3876.

4. *Id.*, p. 3877.

5. *Newdow v. Congress, et al,* No. 06-16344 (9th Cir. 2010), p. 4206.

6. *Newdow v. Bush, 89 Fed.Appx. 624, 625 (9th Cir. 2004); Newdow v. Bush, 391 F.Supp.2d 95, 99-101 (D.D.C. 2005); Newdow v. Roberts, 603 F.3d 1002 (2010).*

7. *Van Orden v. Perry*, 545 U.S. 677 (2005).

8. *McCreary County v. American Civil Liberties Union of Ky.*, 545 U.S. 844 (2005).

9. *Id.*

10. *Cutter v. Wilkinson*, 544 U.S. 709 (2005).

11. *Turner v. Safley*, 482 U.S. 78 (1987).

12. *Hein, Director, White House Office of Faith-Based and Community Initiatives, et al. v. Freedom from Religion Foundation, Inc. et al.,* 551 U.S. 587 (2007) (no standing to bring suit to invalidate Presidential initiative to help faith-based organization compete for federal funding); *Salazar, Secretary of the Interior, et al. v. Buono,* (U.S.S.Ct., April 28,

2010) (suit involving a memorial cross on federal land remanded for further proceedings); *Arizona Christian School Tuition Organization v. Winn et al.,* (U.S.S.Ct., April 4, 2011) (no standing to challenge a state tax credit benefiting religious schools).

13. *Utah Highway Patrol Assn. v. American Atheists, Inc.*, (U.S.S.Ct., October 31, 2011) (cert. denied in 10th Circuit case finding the use of white crosses to mark the locations of the deaths of highway patrol officers was unconstitutional); *Elmbrook School District v. John Doe 3, a Minor by Doe 3's Next Best Friend Doe 2, et al.*, (U.S.S.Ct., June 16, 2014) (cert. denied in 7th Circuit case finding unconstitutional a public school's decision to hold graduation ceremonies in a church).

14. *Utah Highway Patrol Assn.*, id.

15. *Town of Greece, New York v. Galloway et al.*, 572 U.S. 565 (2014).

16. 572 U. S., at ___.

17. 572 U. S., at 576.

18. *American Legion et al. v. American Humanist Assn. et al.*, (U.S.S.Ct., June 20, 2019).

19. Id., Part II B.

20. *Burwell, Secretary of Health and Human Services, et al. v. Hobby Lobby Stores, Inc., et al.*, 573 U.S. ___ (2014).

21. *Employment Division, Department of Human Resources of Oregon v. Smith*, 494 U. S. 872 (1990).

22. Religious Freedom Restoration Act of 1993, 107 Stat. 1488, 42 U. S. C. §2000bb *et seq.*

23. *City of Boerne v. Flores*, 521 U. S. 507, 514 (1997).

24. Religious Land Use and Institutionalized Persons Act of 2000, 114 Stat. 803, 42 U. S. C. §2000cc *et seq.*

25. *Burwell v. Hobby Lobby*, 573 U.S. at ___.

26. *Zubick v. Burwell*, 578 U.S. ___ (2016).

27. *California v. Acosta,* No 19-15072 (9th Cir., October 22, 2019).

28. *Obergefell et al. v. Hodges*, 576 U.S. ___ (2015).

29. Id., 576 U.S. at ___ (Chief Justice Roberts dissenting).

30. Id., 576 U.S. at ___.

31. *Masterpiece Cakeshop v. Colorado Civil Rights Commission*, 584 U.S. ___ (2018).

32. *Arlene's Flowers v. Washington*, No. 17-108 (June 25, 2018).

33. *Masterpiece Cakeshop*, 584 U.S. at ___.

34. Rob Boston, "Washington Officials Not Hostile To Faith In Florist Case, Says State Top Court," *Church & State Magazine*, July/August 2019 <https://www.au.org/church-state/julyaugust-2019-church-state-magazine/people-events/washington-officials-not-hostile>

35. Alexandra Hutzler, "These are all the states that have passed anti-abortion laws in 2019," *Newsweek*, May 31, 2019. <https://www.newsweek.com/state-abortion-laws-2019-list-1440609>

36. "Presidential Executive Order Promoting Free Speech and Religious Liberty," May 4, 2017, <https://www.whitehouse.gov/presidential-actions/presidential-executive-order-promoting-free-speech-religious-liberty/>; "President Donald J. Trump Stands Up For Religious Freedom In The United States," White House Briefing Statement, May 3, 2018. <https://www. whitehouse.gov/briefings-statements/president-donald-j-trump-stands-religious-freedom-united-states/>

37. "Religion," *Gallup*, retrieved December 12, 2019 <http://www.gallup.com/poll/1690/Religion.aspx>

38. Zach Hrynowski, "How Many Americans Believe in God?" Gallup, November 8, 2019 <https://news.gallup.com/poll/268205/americans-believe-god.aspx>

39. "Religion," *Gallup*, retrieved December 12, 2019 <https://news.gallup.com/poll/1690/Religion.aspx>

40. Id.

41. Id.

42. 44 "In U.S., Decline of Christianity Continues at Rapid Pace," *Pew Research Center*, October 17, 2019 < https://www.pewforum.org/2019/10/17/in-u-s-decline-of-christianity-continues-at-rapid-pace/>

43. "Religious Landscape Study," *Pew Research Center*, retrieved December 6, 2019 <http://www.pewforum.org/religious-landscape-study/christians/christian/>;

"U.S. Public Becoming Less Religious," *Pew Research Center*, November 3, 2015 <http://www.pewforum.org/2015/11/03/u-s-public-becoming-less-religious>.

ABOUT THE AUTHOR

Janet Ruth is a former Assistant United States Attorney who has appeared many times before the Ninth Circuit Court of Appeals. She spent several years teaching criminal justice classes, including Constitutional Law, at the college level before taking several years off to raise her two children. After obtaining a master's degree in Biblical Studies, Janet decided to follow her passion for writing and teaching and is currently writing a series of books focused on how Christians can truly live what they say they believe.

Learn more about Janet Ruth at her website: www.JaneTruth.com.

Made in the USA
Monee, IL
19 November 2021

82539233R00083